Alaska's National Parks

PHOTOGRAPHY BY
FRED HIRSCHMANN

TEXT BY
KIM HEACOX

GRAPHIC ARTS CENTER
PUBLISHING COMPANY
PORTLAND, OREGON

ISBN 1-55868-010-1

Library of Congress Number 89-81618

© MCMXC by 1990

Graphic Arts Center Publishing Company

P.O. Box 10306 • Portland, OR 97210

Editor-in-Chief • Douglas A. Pfeiffer

Associate Editor • Jean Andrews

Designer • Robert Reynolds

Cartographer • Manoa Mapworks, Inc.

Typographer • Harrison Typesetting, Inc.

Printer • Moore Lithograph, Inc.

Bindery • Lincoln & Allen

Printed in the United States of America

Third Printing

A s Walt Whitman wrote, "It doesn't take civilization long to use up a continent." From the moment the Mayflower Pilgrims stepped ashore, the American wilderness was doomed. As pioneers, they cleared forests, channeled rivers, drained wetlands, founded cities, won a war, and created a democracy. "The earth is given as a common stock for man to labor and live on," wrote Thomas Jefferson. Given or not, the new Americans took it. A great nation was born, and as it grew so did its appetite. Westward over the Appalachians it expanded, past the Mississippi, across the Great Plains. Cowboys shot buffalo from horseback; gentlemen shot them from railroad cars. Grizzly bears were eradicated, wolves poisoned. Up went barbed wire, down came the American Indian. Might was right, and the land was made safe for cattle and sheep.

Every ten years, the Census Bureau created a map of the contiguous United States, but in 1890, for the first time, the map delineated no frontier. Historian Frederick Jackson Turner warned Congress that this was something to worry about, for the frontier had been the anvil on which our nation had forged her character. Lose it, and we lose a part of ourselves.

Six years later gold was discovered on the Klondike River, and miners, like locusts, swarmed north to the Alaska Territory and the Yukon, bringing with them the same adventure, ambition, and avarice that had "won" the wild West. History, like a folk song, was repeating itself. America's Last Frontier, like her first, began slipping into the bottomless basket of human greed.

As our nation expanded, however, so did our national conscience. New sensibilities evolved, and with them came new analyses of our treatment of the land. Was utility the only measure of its worth? Were we so poor that we needed every acre, or so rich that we did not care? Was America the land of opportunity that could not control her opportunists? Perhaps if a man had two dimes to buy two loaves of bread, he should use one dime to buy one loaf, the other to buy a rose.

In 1872, the creation of Yellowstone National Park—the world's first national park—was an idea as original and transcendental as the idea of democracy itself. While the members of Congress who voted against the bill assured their constituents that few people would ever visit a place so remote as Yellowstone, those who voted for it had a brighter vision for their country and for the world. A century later, the nation would have a National Park System of 330 areas in forty-nine states covering nearly eighty million acres. And more than one hundred other nations would contain some twelve hundred national parks or similar preserves.

In Alaska Territory, the idea germinated with creation of Sitka National Historical Park, followed by establishment of Mount McKinley National Park in 1917, then by Katmai and Glacier Bay national monuments in 1918 and 1925. America's Last Frontier had four roses, and others to follow, but it would take more than half a century to select and establish them.

With the arrival of statehood in 1959, Alaska entered her American adolescence and faced many difficult decisions. Her economy rested on a trinity of timber, fishing, and mining, yet a young tourism industry could be seen on the horizon. Then as now, people recognized not one Alaska but two. The first was for the taking—timber, fish, gold, oil, with hoped-for economic growth, healthy profits, and bumper stickers that said, "More Jobs, Less Wilderness." The other Alaska was for the saving—bears, caribou, moose, wolves, whales, walruses, seals—with entire ecosystems unfenced and sparsely peopled, if peopled at all. Perhaps the world's last, best hope for wilderness.

In 1971, three years after the discovery of oil in Prudhoe Bay, Congress passed the Alaska Native Claims Settlement Act (ANCSA) that bequeathed sizable tracts of land and amounts of money to the Native peoples of Alaska. Across the state, a dozen regional Native corporations were created, and each Native became a shareholder in his or her corporation. Part Magna Carta and part Sword of Damocles, ANCSA was the vehicle that put Native Alaskans on the

Origins

Half Title: *A Dall sheep ram relaxes on Primrose Ridge at Denali National Park.* Frontispiece: *Tundra along the shore of Lower Twin Lake in Lake Clark National Park blazes with fall color.* Left: *A stream empties into the west arm of Glacier Bay.* Above: *Autumn red of alpine bearberry contrasts with the evergreen leaves of lingonberry at Lake Clark National Park.*

road of modern American enterprise. At the same time, however, section 17(d-2) of ANCSA directed the secretary of the interior to identify large tracts of Alaska for consideration as new national parks, monuments, preserves, and refuges.

"A lock-up," grumbled many Alaskans, especially those who had moved up here with their chainsaws and stream dredges to escape bureaucratic restrictions. To them and others like them, including most of the state's political establishment, national parks were an economic death knell. They echoed the same hollow sentiments of lawmakers a century before who had opposed the creation of a park called Yellowstone. But Alaska in 1971 was almost entirely federally owned, not state owned, and it would be the right of every U.S. citizen, Alaskans included, to decide the fate of the so-called d-2 lands. Congress dug in for the fight.

After nine years of legislative battles and midnight compromises, the Alaska National Interest Lands Conservation Act (ANILCA) was signed into law on December 2, 1980. The Louisiana Purchase of the American conservation movement, it more than doubled the acreage of the National Park and National Wildlife Refuge systems. Born that day were seven national parks, ten national preserves, four national monuments, nine national wildlife refuges, and twenty-five wild and scenic rivers. Enlarged were several preexisting areas, including Mount McKinley National Park, renamed Denali National Park and Preserve.

The roll call included Alaska's finest: the temperate rain forests of Admiralty Island and Misty Fiords (administered by the U.S. Forest Service); the human cultures and sweeping lands in Bering Land Bridge, Cape Krusenstern, Kobuk Valley, and Noatak; the shining rivers and imposing peaks of Gates of the Arctic; the peregrine falcons and fire ecology in Yukon-Charley; the azure lakes and sockeye salmon in Katmai and Lake Clark; the "world inside a mountain" in Aniakchak; the glacial legacies in Wrangell-Saint Elias, Kenai Fjords, and Glacier Bay; the wildlife in Denali. To complete the roll call were the preexisting historical parks of Sitka and Klondike Gold Rush. Our nation, still young and exuberant, had been given a second opportunity to save her wilderness heritage on a grand scale, and she had taken it.

The national parks of Alaska are more than pretty places. They are public libraries where every element—flowers, spruce, falcons, moraines, pebbles in a river, the rivers themselves,

 every natural thing—is a book waiting to be read, each a part of a larger story. They speak of ecosystems, Eskimos, balances, biodiversity, and global perspectives. Each area has significant features that elevate its importance and make it unique. But to say one is more attractive than another is folly, as if debasing our appraisal of public lands into a beauty contest. By sheer scope and silence they each bestow on us what John Muir would call "the tonic of wilderness," and Wallace Stegner, "the geography of hope."

Alaska contains two-thirds of the National Park Service lands nationwide, yet receives less than 5 percent of the overall budget. For the cost of one F-15 jet you could operate Noatak National Preserve for 170 years, or Glacier Bay National Park and Preserve for 35 years, or Denali National Park and Preserve for 5 years. Underfunded and understaffed, the National Park Service struggles to manage fifty-four million acres in Alaska—roughly 15 percent of the state—an area half the size of California.

Each park, preserve, and monument has problems, some of them serious, as political favors and small decisions erode them in slow, insidious ways. Alaskans are wiser since 1989 when oil from the *Exxon Valdez* fouled their shores. Said the National Park Service: "The true loss is not one of dollars or individual birds or mammals, but in a radical and uncertain alteration of ecosystems whose integrity had been as uncompromised as any in America."

As large, remote, and rugged as they are, the National Park Service lands in Alaska cannot take care of themselves. They need us, and we need them. Visitation to them tripled from 1981 to 1989, and now, in the twilight decade of the 1990s, a new century marches on the horizon. The future lasts forever, and if we do things right, so will our national parks.

Above: *Alaska blueberries come prewashed on the vine along the shore of Bear Cove, Kenai Fjords National Park.* Pages 8-9: *Thirty-five miles away, the 20,306-foot summit of Mount McKinley (Denali) looms above the rolling hills near Thorofare Pass. Crystal clear skies occur on only a handful of summer days at Denali National Park and Preserve.*

Contents

Near the Teklanika River on a quiet afternoon in Denali National Park and Preserve, a band of Dall sheep ewes graze on the green shoulder of a ridge while their lambs gambol across the flowering carpets of mountain avens and arctic bell heather. The ewes look about, their watchfulness easily mistaken for nonchalance. One of the lambs scampers beneath its mother and peeks out from under her. Fifteen hundred feet below, a shuttle bus rolls by. It is nothing new; the sheep have seen it before.

A cow moose stands amid a forest of spruce, her ears up, her recently born twin calves only a few feet away, her eyes on a yellow shuttle bus rolling by. She has seen it before.

A red fox creeps through willow and dwarf birch, hunting small rodents, then suddenly flushes a ptarmigan that flies across the slope and perches atop a spruce near the road. Not yet fully molted, the ptarmigan—the state bird of Alaska—wears a handsome blend of summer brown and winter white. This particular willow ptarmigan is a male, so recognized by the red comb over its eye. A shuttle bus rolls up and stops. Down go the windows, out come the cameras. The ptarmigan has seen it before. Someone laughs aloud, and the bird flies away.

A grizzly sow lumbers over the tundra, her two cubs trailing behind. They are about six months old and plenty feisty, pawing and snarling at each other like rascals in paradise. Their travels take them up a hillside to a road where a shuttle bus sits idling. The cubs rise up on their hind legs and ogle the bus, something they have never seen before. But mama has. She has seen yellow shuttle buses and blue tour buses her entire life. She pauses on the side of the road, her blond fur so rich it appears to glow from within. She is a Toklat grizzly, a color phase common in the bears of Denali. Her cubs, dark in their youth, will probably grow more blond with age. Two more buses arrive and stop. It is a bear jam, one of many that occur every summer in Denali National Park. Each bus holds about forty people, each of whom strains to get a better view of the bears. Mama and her cubs eventually move upslope and over the ridge, and the people on the buses begin to tell tales they will share for the rest of their lives.

"When Denali National Park shall be made easy of access, with accommodations and facilities for travel . . . it is not difficult to anticipate the enjoyment and inspiration visitors will receive," wrote Charles Sheldon as he camped on the Peters Glacier beneath Mount McKinley in January 1908. It was cold enough to make your teeth ache. Wolves howled. Ravens called. The tracks of moose, fox, hare, lynx, and ptarmigan appeared here and there. Sheldon mushed sled dogs over the white wilderness and loved every minute of it. A member of the influential Boone and Crocket Club, he returned home to the East Coast determined to make Denali a national park. It was not easy, but after nine years of legislative debate and compromise, culminating in a congressional bill in February of 1917, Sheldon hand-delivered it for signature to President Woodrow Wilson, thus creating Mount McKinley National Park, the premier national park in Alaska.

Enlarged to six million acres and renamed Denali National Park and Preserve in 1980, Denali receives more visitors than any other national park in Alaska. It is precisely what Charles Sheldon predicted: the state's premier tourist destination and "enjoyment and inspiration" for hundreds of thousands of visitors each year.

"A Subarctic Serengeti," people have called it, and "the Africa of America." Denali has had its share of epithets, most of them exaggerations—but excusable exaggerations—for a single journey through here can do wonders for the human spirit. Take the bus trip to Wonder Lake, a five-hour, eighty-five-mile trip on a winding dirt road through some of the grandest scenery and wildlife habitat in Interior Alaska. You will end up tender in the derriere, but richer in the heart. And crowning the park will be the mountain called McKinley, or, more accurately, Denali—an Athabascan word meaning the "high one"—the highest peak in North America, 20,306 feet above sea level. In this park there are mountains, and

Denali

Left: *The setting sun illuminates lenticular clouds and the tip of Mount McKinley two hundred forty miles south of the Arctic Circle. The curvature of the earth just keeps the rays of the midnight sun from striking the mountaintop on the longest day of the year.* Above: *Lapland rosebay blooms among boughs of white spruce at the base of Cathedral Mountain.*

there is "the mountain." The mountains themselves are impressive ramparts of ice, rock, and snow, but McKinley stands head and shoulders above them all.

About one thousand mountaineers from around the world test their mettle on the mountain every year. Most fly by ski plane from Talkeetna to the seventy-five-hundred foot level of the Kahiltna Glacier, on the mountain's south side. From there the long walk begins.

The odds are that about 50 percent will reach the summit, and a small number will die. The mountain takes prisoners with storms that trap climbers for days in their tents or in snow caves at fourteen- and seventeen thousand feet. The storm might break, and the climbers might reach the summit amid spectacular light and scenery, or they might contract cerebral or pulmonary edema and need to get downslope as quickly as possible.

Why do they climb the mountain? "If you have to ask," they say, "you'll never know." Mountaineer and author Jonathan Waterman wrote in *High Alaska*, "I have witnessed climbers, like prospectors of an earlier era, who staked their fortunes, sacrificed their careers, and left their loved ones to climb these peaks. Some reach the summit and some do not. Some get frostbitten, rescued, or even killed. But more than a few come out with a new gleam in their eyes, as if they, too, had discovered gold."

Denali National Park and Preserve is the size of Massachusetts. The park has dozens of excellent hiking routes, as well as 37 species of mammals, 155 species of birds, and more than 450 species of plants. There are ridges, rivers, valleys, taiga, and tundra to explore. Yet most visitors climb aboard a bus and stay there as though their lives depended on it, climbing off only at rest stops and at the Eielson Visitor Center. The park charms them but intimidates them as well. They are more comfortable viewing things from behind a window, surrounded by their own kind.

The buses have obvious advantages. By accommodating large numbers of visitors they minimize traffic and disturbance of wildlife along the road. Furthermore, visitors on buses see more wildlife than do those in private cars. Forty pairs of eyes simultaneously scan the landscape, and when one passenger sees an animal and alerts the driver, the bus stops and everyone sees it. And though it is difficult to prove, wildlife biologists strongly suspect that if

buses were replaced by private cars, the increased traffic would displace wildlife along the road.

Here, then, that old conundrum raises its ugly head, the one about a beautiful place that someone discovers and announces to the world, and everyone flocks there until it is beautiful no more. In 1971, Denali had thirty thousand visitors; nearly twenty years later it had six hundred thousand. How much is too much? Charles Sheldon would be astounded, perhaps even dismayed, for Denali is not the same roadless, peopleless place he discovered in 1908. Still beautiful? Yes. But not the same.

Sandhill cranes still fly overhead every September. Wolves still patrol the Toklat River. Gyrfalcons and golden eagles still sail off the cliffs of Polychrome Pass, while caribou migrate through the park between wintering and calving grounds, and bears still cause the world's most fascinating traffic jams along the road at Sable Pass. It is a magnificent park—so vast and wild yet accessible. But if its doors were opened to every visitor who came knocking, and if visitation quadrupled in the next twenty years, what would become of the wildlife? Or of the park's wilderness integrity? Can we afford to find out?

"The national park idea represents a far-reaching cultural achievement, for here we raise our thoughts above the average, and enter a sphere in which the intangible values of the human heart and spirit take precedence," wrote wildlife biologist Adolf Murie. "All the plants and animals enjoy a natural and normal life without human restrictions. . . . Our task is to perpetuate this freedom and purity of nature, this ebb and flow of life—first, by insuring ample park boundaries so that the region is large enough to maintain the natural relationships, and secondly, to hold man's intrusions to a minimum."

Above: *A bull caribou's antlers are covered with rich velvet in August.* Right: *A caribou antler dropped the previous year rests on a bed of lichen and alpine bearberry east of Wonder Lake. Shed antlers become an important source of calcium for porcupines, arctic ground squirrels, and other small mammals. Over the years, antlers are often completely gnawed away.*

■ *Left:* Although the snows have melted, a male rock ptarmigan still sports his white plummage. In a few weeks most of his feathers will moult to mottled brown, matching the color of alpine tundra. ■ *Above:* A bull caribou surveys his domain above fog-shrouded McKinley River. Estimated at twenty thousand in 1940, the Denali Caribou Herd crashed to approximately one thousand individuals by 1977 and has slowly rebounded to about three thousand today.

■ *Above:* Spring melt from snow and glaciers swells the braided channels of the Toklat River. Fording swollen glacial rivers is a danger perhaps as great as that posed by grizzly bears in Denali's back country. ■ *Right:* A favorite haunt of hoary marmots, Marmot Hill rises above gravel stream-beds wending their way from the Alaska Range. The view from Polychrome Pass is one of the finest on the eighty-five mile length of the park road.

■ *Left:* In late August and early September, foliage of alpine bearberry and blueberries radiates autumnal splendor. The land blazes but briefly in a riot of color before winter applies its forceful grip. ■ *Above:* On a grander scale, the setting sun's rays paint the peaks of the Alaska Range above Gorge Creek in crimson light. ■ *Following Pages:* As sunset progresses, it spotlights only the highest peaks south of Eielson, revealing fresh snow of fall's first storm.

■ *Above:* A cow moose and her calf browse on willow shoots near Hines Creek. In recent years, grizzly bears have taken a heavy toll of the moose calves during their first few weeks of life. ■ *Right:* Appropriately named Denali, meaning "the high one," by the Athabascans of Interior Alaska, Mount McKinley crowns the continent as North America's highest peak. West of Eielson, numerous ponds and lakes reflect the mountain on calm days.

I f the Ice Age is still alive, yet banished, its glaciers lurking in the highest mountains and polar regions, just waiting to readvance over the temperate world, and if you want to seek those glaciers in their hiding place, consider exploring Wrangell-Saint Elias National Park and Preserve. Of the more than three hundred units in the U.S. National Park Service System, 13.2-million-acre Wrangell-Saint Elias is the largest. Nearly six Yellowstones would fit into it.

Fly over it and you see mountains beyond mountains, rivers after rivers, glaciers after glaciers. "People have tried to quantify this immensity," wrote historian William E. Brown in *This Last Treasure*. "The parkland contains nine peaks more than 14,000 feet high, four of them rising more than 16,000 feet. There are uncounted peaks in the 10,000 to 14,000-foot range. Storms annually precipitate as much as 50 feet of snow in the upper reaches of the Saint Elias chain and along the Bagley Icefield. The compacting loads of snow feed 75 named glaciers and many unnamed. The Bering and Nabesna are among the world's longest glaciers. The Malaspina is one of the world's largest piedmont or lowland glaciers. The glaciers, in turn, generate the two dozen river systems that drain the parkland."

The biggest, the highest, the longest—so it goes in this corner of Alaska. You could fly over it for hours—for days, in fact—and continue to see new country. "I've been here for nine years," says district ranger and park pilot Jim Hannah, "and every time I go out I learn something and gain a better understanding of the land. There's so much to learn here, the land is so vast and complex, you could spend a lifetime figuring it all out, and if you did there'd still be more to see and do."

Four major Alaskan mountain ranges—the Wrangell, the Saint Elias, the Chugach, and the Alaskan—converge in this park, and with them converge the ranges of certain species of wildlife. Dall sheep and mountain goats, mutually exclusive in most places, can be found grazing on the same slopes near the headwaters of the Chitina River and elsewhere. The Wrangell Mountains alone contain more than ten thousand Dall sheep, the only wild white species of sheep in the world. The broad, gracefully sweeping horns of the rams make them favorite targets of sports hunters and photographers, though while one kills the ram and hangs its head on a wall, the other takes a picture and leaves the ram where he found him—in the mountains of Alaska. Unlike antlers (found on caribou, moose, deer, and elk) which are shed and grown anew each year, horns are retained for life. Count the growth rings, like the rings on a tree, and you will know the ram's age. Mountain goats also have horns, though smaller, and if the truth be known, they are not goats at all but actually mountain antelopes and close relatives of the chamois of Europe. Whereas Dall sheep predominate to the north in the Wrangell Mountains, mountain goats predominate to the south in the Saint Elias Range, the tallest coastal mountains in the world. In the heart of the park where the two great ranges converge, so do the sheep and goats.

Other wildlife live here as well. Moose, wolves, beavers, wolverines, grizzlies, martens, and golden eagles thrive inland, while along the coast amid the tides and icebergs of Icy Bay, Yakutat Bay, and the Malaspina forelands are sea lions, harbor seals, bald eagles, and the rare glacier bear, a blue-gray phase of the black bear seldom seen elsewhere in Alaska. And crowning it all only fifteen miles from Icy Bay is the 18,008-foot summit of Mount Saint Elias, the third highest mountain in North America (behind Mounts McKinley and Logan).

Though wildlife adds an important dimension, and summer wildflowers throw vibrant colors across the alpine slopes, it is the topography itself that truly defines Wrangell-Saint Elias. For anyone wishing to stand atop summits where no one has stood before, and to risk life and limb doing it, this is your park. A flatlander might faint here, while a glaciologist—one who studies rivers of ice, especially alpine rivers of ice—would be like a kid in a candy store.

Left: *Deep in the Wrangell Mountains, a field of glacial erratics and pioneering dryas speak of the recent retreat of the Kuskalana Glacier. Only a few miles away, fresh snow caps a peak high above Nugget Creek. Above: Overburden, which was removed from the copper mines at Kennicott, is hidden behind the dense foliage of the northern red currant.*

Volcanics and tectonic plates created the Wrangell, Saint Elias, Chugach, and Alaskan mountains, but more recently, in the last million years or so, glaciers carved and shaped them. Fly over this country and you will see countless examples of textbook glaciation; of ice grinding rock into silt; of V-shaped valleys becoming U-shaped valleys; of moraines, cols, arêtes, kame terraces, kettle ponds, horns, erratics, eskers, crevasses, turbid rivers, and even rock glaciers—each a signature that when added to the others creates a composite picture of how ice shaped this land and continues to shape it. "I might be slow," a glacier mused in a cartoonist's rendering, "but I'm inexorable."

Some are not even slow. In 1986, the Hubbard Glacier surged forward and occluded Russell Fjord from Disenchantment Bay in the southeast corner of the park. Thus separated from the ocean, Russell Fjord filled with fresh water and became a lake, endangering seals and porpoises trapped there. Biologists tried and failed to rescue the animals, and the media arrived to tell the world all about it. Finally, after the lake had risen eighty-three feet in six months, the ice dam broke and the water drained in less than a day, pouring back into the sea with a force estimated at thirty-five times greater than the power of Niagara Falls. The press said things were back to normal, yet a couple of years later the Hubbard Glacier was once again threatening to occlude Russell Fjord. In glacier country like this, the only thing "normal" is change itself.

This land might sound so wild and rugged as to be utterly peopleless, but it is not, for amid the mountains, ice, and flowers lives a sprinkling of humanity every bit as colorful as the surrounding land. The Wrangell Mountains had been home to the Ahtna Athabascans long before miners first trickled into the country around the turn of the century, and when gold and copper were discovered, the trickle became a torrent. The copper deposit above the Kennicott Glacier was proclaimed the "richest in the world." From 1911 to 1938 the Kennecott Mining Company extracted 591,000 tons of copper and 900,000 ounces of silver, and corporate profits soared above two hundred million dollars. The mine site is inactive now, but the buildings, still dressed in striking red paint with white trim, are among the most photogenic in Alaska.

Today, the old communities of Nabesna and McCarthy still wear the faces of mining, but also the faces of those who have settled here for nothing more than the solitude and the pace of life. In 1979, while public hearings discussed the imminent creation of Wrangell-Saint Elias National Park and Preserve, the McCarthy Community Council delivered this self-portrait: "We are a diverse and dynamic group of people, no more or less than people anywhere else. Yet it can be said that the sometimes harsh environment in which we build our homes, hunt, and gather wood has made us keenly aware of the sensitivities and limits of this area. Learning to live and accept these limits has woven us into the fabric of nature's tapestry just as surely as the animals and trees." Another resident, when asked why he lived in the Wrangells, reportedly said, "Go take a walk fifteen miles into the wilderness, and go out and see the land, interview a moose. Then perhaps you'll understand why I am here."

Photographer Fred Hirschmann and I failed to interview a moose in the Wrangell Mountains, but we found an ice cave in the Kennicott Glacier and crawled inside for a better look. It seemed a fitting way to end our visit in a park sculpted by glacial ice. Images of *20,000 Leagues Under the Sea* came to us as we entered the wet, blue world and stood amid the scalloped walls and the timbre of dripping water. "Magical" describes it best, for I can think of nothing else like it. We could have been killed but were not, and the moment we stepped back into the brilliant sunshine, feasting our eyes on the grand scenery 360 degrees around, we drank a toast to the tonic of wilderness and the art of adventure. And only then did we head for home.

Above: *An estimated ten- to twelve thousand Dall sheep call Wrangell-Saint Elias home.* Right: *Dark stripes of rubble—medial moraines—meander down Russell Glacier. Snow feeding the glacier falls on the University Range, of which Mount Churchill and Mount Bona are visible.* Following Pages: *Mount Blackburn towers over the silty waters of Kuskalana River.*

■ *Left:* Rising thirteen stories, the Kennecott Mining Company's copper mill gradually succumbs to the elements. From 1906 to 1938, 591,000 tons of copper and 900,000 ounces of silver were processed by the mill. ■ *Above:* An eerie blue light radiates from the sculpted walls of an ice cave incised in the Kennicott Glacier. Stagnant ice is conducive to the formation of ice caves. Their exploration is dangerous, for falling ice and rocks pose constant threats.

■ *Above:* Dan Creek joins twisted channels of the Nizina River. Fed predominately by glaciers, the silty rivers of Wrangell-Saint Elias National Park and Preserve exhibit considerable change in their day-to-day flow. Warm days melt glacial ice with subsequent run-off swelling the rivers. ■ *Right:* Southeast of Chitistone River, the rugged peaks of the University Range are capped with glacial ice. Nearby Goat Trail attracts only a handful of hikers each year.

Twelve hundred miles from where it empties into the Bering Sea, the Yukon River slides past the town of Eagle, near the United States/Canada International Boundary, and enters Yukon-Charley Rivers National Preserve. A great wide river, it flows past towering bluffs and boreal forests. Called the "Route 66 of the North," it is the largest river running through a National Park Service area. Dog mushers and snowmobilers travel by winter; boaters, rafters, canoeists, and kayakers by summer. Float the river and camp on an island; mush dogs over the cold, white silence and come around a bend to find a cabin in the woods like something out of *The Spell of the Yukon* by Robert Service:

The strong life that knows no harness; The wilds where the caribou call
The freshness, the freedom, the farness—O God, how I'm stuck on it all!

Midway along its 128-mile journey through the preserve, the Yukon is joined by the Charley, flowing in from the south. Three-quarters of the preserve is spruce forest; the rest, upland tundra and rock. Mining brought the people here, mostly, and though the old mining days add historical color, contemporary mining threatens the preserve. The dredges are bigger now and more destructive. Within the 2.52-million-acre preserve are 300,000 acres of selected or conveyed lands, many of which could be opened to mining.

Steve Ulvi came into this country in 1974, lived along the river and trapped, then moved into Eagle and was hired by the National Park Service as a resource management specialist. "This is a place of subtle values," he says. "One of the best kept secrets in the Park Service . . . a place to dally and look around and learn. . . ."

Fire and ice interplay in fascinating ways here. Much of the preserve was not glaciated during the last Ice Age and thus represents an eastern Beringia, a refugia where pockets of vegetation exist unlike any other. Add a complex fire history atop underlying permafrost and you get what Ulvi calls "a plant ecology as interesting as any place else in Alaska. There's hardly a place you can go in this preserve and not find evidence of fire."

It is a place to hear wolves howl and thrushes sing; to bask in wilderness and hear yourself think. "[Eagle and Circle] are about a hundred and sixty river miles apart, and in all the land between them live perhaps thirty people," wrote John McPhee in *Coming Into the Country.*
"The State of New Jersey . . . could fit between Eagle and Circle. New Jersey has seven and a half million people. Small wonder that the Alaskan wild has at least a conceptual appeal to certain people from a place like New Jersey."

So McPhee headed down the mighty Yukon: "We picked our way through flights of wooded islands. We shivered in the deep shadows of bluffs a thousand feet high—Calico Bluff, Montauk Bluff, Biederman Bluff, Takoma Bluff—which day after day intermittently walled the river. Between them— in downpourings of sunshine, as often as not—long vistas reached back across spruce-forested hills to the rough gray and freshly whitened summits of mountains. Some of the walls of the bluffs were of dark igneous rock that had cracked into bricks. . . . Peregrine falcons nest there, and—fantastic flyers—will come over the Yukon at ballastic speeds, clench  their talons, tuck them in, and strike a flying duck hard enough (in the neck) to kill it in midair. End over end the duck falls, and the falcon catches it before it hits the river."

Fifty to sixty pairs of peregrines, probably the largest breeding population in a federally protected area, breed in Yukon-Charley Rivers. An endangered species, the peregrine has come to symbolize the wild heart of this country as much as the rivers. Yet these flyers spend only part of the year here, traveling as far south as Mexico for the winter. What happens to them down there is unknown, but one thing is certain: they are not as well protected.

Like all preserves, parks, monuments, and wildlife refuges in Alaska, Yukon-Charley Rivers flows with the tides of global change. Its boundaries reflect ecosystems and drainages in some areas; political gerrymandering in others. Yet the rivers roll on, and with them the rhythms of fire, falcons, ice, and water, all beneath the subarctic skies of Eastern Alaska.

Yukon-Charley Rivers

Left: *Inactive since 1975, a huge gold dredge stands on Coal Creek, a Yukon River tributary. The mechanical monster could handle 3,000 cubic yards of gravel a day, worth about 20 to 25 cents per cubic yard.* Above: *Siberian aster blooms by the Yukon River.* Following Pages: *The Tatonduk River flows from the Ogilvie Mountains past Nimrod Peak and Squaw Mountain.*

■ *Left:* All the gold that glitters in Yukon-Charley is not necessarily in placer deposits hidden beneath stream gravels. Tumbling waters of the Tatonduk River glisten with golden splendor at sunset. ■ *Above:* Mist rises from the Yukon River on a chilly September morning. The placid Yukon is interior Alaska's water highway. Stretching 1,979 miles from headwaters in Canada to its mouth on the Bering Sea, the mighty Yukon divides Alaska roughly in half.

■ *Above:* At Calico Bluff, the Yukon River's erosive action exposes inter-bedded layers of limestone and shale, contorted by pressures from within the earth. Numerous marine fossils speak of a shallow sea here approximately 330 million years ago. ■ *Right:* Dick Cook pauses during gardening at his homestead in Yukon-Charley Rivers National Preserve. Alaska's new national parks allow rural residents to continue their traditional subsistence lifestyle.

Henry David Thoreau had his Walden Pond, John Muir his Yosemite Valley, and Robert Marshall what later became Gates of the Arctic National Park and Preserve. Hiking up the North Fork of the Koyukuk River in the Central Brooks Range in late July 1929, Marshall scrambled up a hill and beheld a view he shared with the world. "The view from the top gave us an excellent idea of the jagged country toward which we were heading," he wrote. "The main Brooks Range divide was entirely covered with snow. Close at hand, only about ten air miles to the north, was a precipitous pair of mountains, one on each side of the North Fork. I bestowed the name Gates of the Arctic on them, christening the east portal Boreal Mountain and the west portal Frigid Crags."

For the next ten years, Robert Marshall let this wild, rocky land seep into him. Finally headed home to the East Coast, he wrote, "In a day I should be in Fairbanks, in two more in Juneau, in a week in Seattle and the great, thumping, modern world." But was he really heading home, or leaving it? For the realization was upon him that, ". . . no comfort, no security, no invention, no brilliant thought which the modern world had to offer could provide half the elation of the days spent in the little explored, uninhabited world of the arctic wilderness."

Without so much as blinking, Marshall suggested that all of Alaska from the Brooks Range north be preserved as wilderness. "How much wilderness do we need?" someone once asked him. "How many Brahms symphonies do we need?" he replied.

He died in 1939 at the age of thirty-eight. Today his vision of an entire Arctic Alaska wilderness is lost. America decided oil was more important. Yet the place most dear to him, the Central Brooks Range, is preserved in Gates of the Arctic National Park and Preserve.

It is a big park and has to be, for life is thin, and ecosystems are large above the Arctic Circle. Tundra spreads over the land like a living skin on cold, hard rock. Climb a ridge and look around and you might see half a dozen glacial cirques rimmed by cliffs and buttressed by talus. An old pair of caribou antlers lies in the tundra where it has lain for years, perhaps for decades, partly buried in arctic bell heather, mosses, and lichens. Mountain avens and moss campion grow nearby. A storm brews in one end of the valley, near the crest of the Brooks Range, while sunshine spills into the other, its light dancing off a distant river. You expect a rainbow, but the storm moves your way and hails right on top of you. Hail in July. An hour later, it has ended, the sunshine is back, and you stumble through the tussocks down to the river where your friends have pitched camp. The next morning when you awaken and peek outside, fresh grizzly tracks circle your tent. So it goes in one of the last great wild places in the world.

Six officially designated wild and scenic rivers have their headwaters here, each arising from the Continental Divide and crest of the ancient Brooks Range, the northernmost mountain range in the world. The Kobuk and Noatak Rivers flow west to the Chukchi Sea. The Alatna, John, and Tinayguk rivers, and the North Fork of the Koyukuk flow south into the Yukon and eventually into the Bering Sea. Caribou, grizzlies, Eskimos, and Athabascans have followed these rivers for ages; contemporary recreationists, their numbers increasing every year, have followed them for decades. They often float for a day and hike for a day, over and over until their anxieties wash away in the clear, cold water. Perhaps they will see a gyrfalcon plummet into a ptarmigan, a grizzly chase a ground squirrel, or a shaft of midnight sunlight hit the peaks with brilliant oranges and reds. Or it might rain the entire trip. Either way, time is not on a wristwatch here; it is the river running, the lichens growing, the thunder and silence and wind in an untrammeled land that inspires you one minute, humbles you the next. You return to the modern world, as Robert Marshall did, wondering about the so-called merits of civilization.

Sigurd Olson, former president of the Wilderness Society and the National Parks and Conservation Association, once wrote, "All Alaska has an early morning freshness for me.

Gates of the Arctic

Left: *In the 8.4 million acres of Gates of the Arctic National Park and Preserve, a nameless river winds through a nameless valley that is surrounded by nameless limestone spires.* Above: *The early summer wildflower show in the Brooks Range peaks just as droves of mosquitoes appear. Here, mountain avens bloom against a backdrop of black oxytropes.*

While it is not young, and some of its ranges are as ancient as any on earth, I cannot help but feel when I see such mountains as the Brooks, that this is how the Appalachians, the Rockies and the Laurentians once were. With that realization I somehow see, with greater understanding, the long road over which not only mountains, but all life has come. Such places answer a question for me that has reverberated down through the centuries: 'When I consider thy heavens, the work of thy fingers, the moon and the stars, which thou hast ordained; What is man, that thou art mindful of him?'"

For all its ruggedness, Gates of the Arctic is a fragile place. A contradictory place. The land intimidates, yet inspires; you grow humble, yet confidant; things live and die. A patch of tundra that takes a century to pioneer a ridge can be scuffed away in a moment beneath the fancy boot of an insensitive hiker.

Only a few years after the establishment of the park in 1980, trails—the signatures of parks elsewhere in the nation but not in Alaska—began to appear. Hiking here is not a single-file affair but a chance to emulate the land and spread out, to practice reverence, to partake of the silence, and to tread as lightly as possible.

The Eskimos have descriptive names for every time of year here. May is the month-of-fawning; June, egg-month; July, mosquito-month; and August, berry-month. "There is, to be sure, a kind of biotic riot in the summer outburst of color, scent and sound," wrote David Roberts, "But always the season's opposite haunts you: what about winter? What must that be like?"

In his book, *Going to Extremes*, Joe McGinness describes a hike in Gates of the Arctic with several companions. One of those companions was Ray Bane, a park ranger and former schoolteacher who mushed dogs in the Brooks Range and would someday become superintendent of Katmai National Park. "We stopped for a late morning rest," wrote Joe McGinness. "The sun was so strong, the air still so warm, that we took off our shirts and let them dry, and sat, bare-chested, feeling the soft breeze cool our skin. It did not seem possible that we were one hundred miles above the Arctic Circle. 'All this is a lie,' Ray Bane said. 'A beautiful lie. Winter is the truth about Alaska.'"

Where the mountains break their backs against the sky, a few summits have familiar names—Arrigetch, Doonerak, Igikpak, Frigid Crags, and Boreal Mountain—yet most are nameless and will remain that way, for this is not a Brave New World in the technological termitarium of modern man, but a rhythmic, balanced, ancient place with its Arctic metronome set to the harmony of caribou and lichen, erosion and deposition, tundra and taiga, Dall sheep and wolves, summer and winter. Go out there and see for yourself.

"Adventure," wrote Marshall, "whether physical or mental, implies breaking into unpenetrated ground, venturing beyond the boundary of normal aptitude, extending oneself to the limit of capacity, courageously facing peril. Life without the chance for such exertions would be for many persons a dreary game, scarcely bearable in its horrible banality."

In the summer of 1986, fifty-some-odd years after Robert Marshall penned those words, park ranger Richard Steele solo hiked 104 miles in six days from Wiseman to Anaktuvuk Pass through the eastern half of the Gates of the Arctic National Park. "The fear of bears is a wonderful thing," he told me after the trip. He forded rivers, climbed ridges, bashed willow, found moose, flushed ptarmigan, hiked past midnight, slept past noon, and saw not a single bear. "They were out there," he said. "I just didn't see any, but they probably saw me. It was a hard hike. The weather was bad, and my feet swelled up, and I caught a fever the last day. But I made it and I consider myself lucky to have walked in one the world's few remaining places where you can learn humility and respect from grizzly bears. That means a lot to me."

It meant a lot to Robert Marshall, too.

Above: *A caribou antler rests on a bed of lichens and willows in the Endicott Mountains. Gates of the Arctic protects vast habitat critical to the Western Arctic Caribou Herd.* Right: *August snow dusts a meadow rimmed with limestone cliffs and spires as a lone mew gull flies in stormy skies. The Brooks Range is the northernmost extent of the Rocky Mountains.*

■ *Left:* Orange cement binds former stream gravels into a colorful conglomerate boulder. The Endicott Mountains hold innumerable surprises. ■ *Above:* Morning light reflects the Arrigetch Peaks off Arrigetch Creek. Most of the Brooks Range is composed of sedimentary rock. However, at the Arrigetch, the granitic core of the range is exposed. Glacial carving and the slightly curving exfoliation peculiar to granite has sculpted cliffs, domes, and knife ridges.

■ *Above:* A willow struggles for existence on a rocky ridge among the granite mountains. The veneer of vegetation in the Arrigetch holds a tenuous grip on life. A hiker's misplaced foot can destroy lichens that have taken 150 years to mature. The 8.4 million acres of Gates of the Arctic National Park and Preserve provide ample room for visitors to spread out. ■ *Right:* One of twelve drainages departing the Arrigetch, Arrigetch Creek tumbles into a rocky chasm.

■ *Left:* Black granite fangs gnaw toward arctic skies. Remnants of a body of magma that cooled 360 to 440 million years ago, the Arrigetch contains some of Alaska's most spectacular and rugged scenery. ■ *Above:* Swollen by a summer thunderstorm, Contact Creek cascades from the Endicott Mountains toward Anaktuvuk Pass and John River. Thick brush and unstable clumps of sedges and grasses, called tussocks, impede hiking on the valley floor.

H aving chased the ghosts of glaciers in the Sierra Nevada for ten years, John Muir came to what would become Glacier Bay National Park and Preserve to chase the glaciers themselves. It was October 1879, the rainiest month of the year, when the indefatigable forty-one-year-old Muir bounded off a steamer in Fort Wrangell with hardtack in his pockets and mischief in his eyes. A few days later, he secured a canoe and the company of a Presbyterian minister and four Tlingit Indians. They paddled north into mysterious waters, and the farther north they went, the more mysterious the waters became. Rain fell daily. Temperatures dropped. Yet up in the bow sat Muir, urging his companions onward, his beard waving in the wind, his eyes the color of glacial ice, his heart pulled into country most men would avoid.

Two hundred miles north of Fort Wrangell they entered Icy Strait and stopped at the Tlingit village of Hoonah, on the north side of Chichagof Island. There the local Tlingits spoke about a bay across the strait where giant ice rivers moved over land and sea; a bay of white thunder and perilous waters where forests once grew but were destroyed by the ice.

Muir listened. Could this have been the same bay explored eighty-five years earlier, in 1794, by Lieutenants Whidbey and LeMesurier serving under Captain George Vancouver? Commanding HMS *Discovery*, Vancouver had dropped anchor near Cross Sound, where Icy Strait enters the Gulf of Alaska, and sent his longboats and lieutenants eastbound through fog and uncharted waters. They found Taylor and Dundas bays and, beyond them, another bay which Vancouver later described as about five miles long and "terminated by compact solid mountains of ice, rising perpendicularly from the water's edge, and bounded to the north by a continuation of the united lofty frozen mountains that extend eastward from Mount Fairweather." Vancouver further reported "great quantities of broken ice, which having been put in motion by the springing up of a northerly wind, was drifted to the southward. . . ."

Paddling north out of Hoonah, Muir could harldly believe his eyes, for the bay Vancouver described in 1794 as about five miles long was now, in 1879, more than thirty miles long. Though it appeared Vancouver might have miscalculated, he did not. A former midshipman and student of cartography under Captain James Cook, he had developed a penchant for

meticulous mapping. His charts of 1794 were accurate but not for long, for unbeknownst to Vancouver, he, like Muir, had stumbled upon the most rapid glacial retreat ever recorded. In fact, Vancouver's maps initiate a record of that retreat, for what he described in 1794 as "compact solid mountains of ice, rising perpendicularly from the water's edge" was the terminus of a massive tidewater glacier that filled Glacier Bay, a terminus perhaps three hundred feet high, six miles across, and five miles back from the mouth of the bay we know today.

If the first chapter of discovery goes to Vancouver and his lieutenants, the second belongs to John Muir, archdruid, naturalist, lightning rod among early environmentalists and, as he would later describe himself, "an author and student of glaciers." For ten years he had hiked California's Sierra Nevada, observing striations, pluckings, moraines, till, kettle ponds, and other geomorphological clues—the ghosts of glaciers—which convinced him Yosemite Valley had been created by glaciers, not by faulting. Announcing this, he was ridiculed by the scientific community. So the blue-eyed explorer came to Alaska, not for gold or timber or fish, but for wealth of a different kind—scenery, inspiration, and, of course, glaciers. He would not be disappointed.

Paddling into the bay until the icebergs grew too thick to continue, the party went ashore in the vicinity of Hugh Miller Inlet, and without wasting a heartbeat, Muir headed upslope. "Climbing higher for still a broader outlook," he wrote, "I made precious time while sunshine streamed through the luminous fringes of the clouds and fell on the glittering bergs, the crystal bluffs of the two vast glaciers, and the intensely white, far-spreading fields of ice, and the ineffably chaste and spiritual heights of the Fairweather Range, which were now

Left: *The scores of glaciers in 3.3-million-acre Glacier Bay National Park and Preserve evoke a sense of primordial North America. It is dangerous to walk inside a glacier, but its icy world hints of unearthly dimensions. Spectacular caves melt through stagnant ice isolated from the mass of a glacier. Above: Rosy sunset light illuminates snow-capped peaks east of Muir Inlet.*

Glacier Bay

hidden, now partly revealed, the whole making a picture of icy wildness unspeakably pure and sublime."

John Muir had found Glacier Bay, an open book on the last Ice Age. The great glacier recorded by Vancouver's lieutenants in 1794 had retreated and split into two main tributaries: one, today called Muir Glacier, thirty miles up the bay on the east side; the other, today called Grand Pacific Glacier, fifty miles up the bay on the west side. Muir was ecstatic, for here the grand processes of geology were condensed into a human time frame, occurring in years rather than in millennia. In a single lifetime, one could watch a mountain or a ridge or an entire bay emerge from under a shrinking sheet of ice. Here glaciers were not only to be found, they were extremely active, pouring out of the mountains to the sea where they would calve great shards of ice that hit the water with the force of cannonballs. "White thunder," the Tlingits called it.

More than a century after Muir's visit, Glacier Bay still resounds with white thunder. The Muir Glacier has retreated another twenty-five miles, opening up Muir Inlet, while glaciers in the bay's west arm, having reached their maximum retreat a few decades ago, sixty-five miles from the mouth of the bay, now threaten to advance. More than a dozen tidewater glaciers occupy the bay today, each sequestered at the back of an inlet.

Muir, Margerie, McBride, Reid, Riggs, Rendu, Grand Pacific, Johns Hopkins reads the roll call of these rivers of ice. Standing on a cruise ship or sitting in a kayak, you can wait for hours for them to calve. They have more patience than we do. Then again, the white thunder might resound several times an hour, the ice shards falling, splashing, and sending waves down the inlets. Harbor seals gather on the icebergs, kittiwakes nest on the cliffs, bears patrol the shoreline. All in a land buried by one massive glacier thousands of feet thick, and not that long ago.

As the great ice sheet retreated, sunlight and rain fell upon the land for the first time in perhaps five- to eight thousand years. Sometime back then, the bay resembled the Glacier Bay we know: inlets, forests, wildlife, mountains, and glaciers. But the climate changed, and the glaciers advanced and merged and filled the bay. Then two hundred years ago, about the

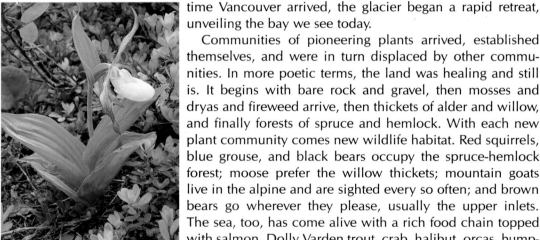

time Vancouver arrived, the glacier began a rapid retreat, unveiling the bay we see today.

Communities of pioneering plants arrived, established themselves, and were in turn displaced by other communities. In more poetic terms, the land was healing and still is. It begins with bare rock and gravel, then mosses and dryas and fireweed arrive, then thickets of alder and willow, and finally forests of spruce and hemlock. With each new plant community comes new wildlife habitat. Red squirrels, blue grouse, and black bears occupy the spruce-hemlock forest; moose prefer the willow thickets; mountain goats live in the alpine and are sighted every so often; and brown bears go wherever they please, usually the upper inlets. The sea, too, has come alive with a rich food chain topped with salmon, Dolly Varden trout, crab, halibut, orcas, humpback whales, harbor seals, and—more recently—Steller sea lions. Add to that several seabird colonies and a full complement of land birds.

Where once only white thunder echoed through a lifeless land, today wolves howl, seals growl, whales feed, and birds sing. Luxury cruise ships enter the bay, and kayakers paddle amid the poetry of running tides. John Muir and George Vancouver would be astounded, for the pendulum of change has swung high and far. The glaciers have retreated, and a bay has been born. Yet if we could visit Glacier Bay two hundred years from now, the surprise might be ours, for change is the only constant. The glaciers, like the tides, have ebbed and flowed here many times over the last two million years and will probably do so again. Perhaps the climate will shift, precipitation will increase, and glaciers will reclaim the bay, for a pendulum can stay at the top of its arc only so long before it swings back.

Above: A yellow lady's slipper blooms near the base of Gloomy Knob. Right: Sunset reflects in the peaceful water of a tidal pond along the west arm of Glacier Bay. When Captain George Vancouver explored Icy Strait in 1794, Glacier Bay was a mere indentation. Behind stretched a river of ice, nearly fifteen miles wide, five thousand feet deep, and one hundred miles long.

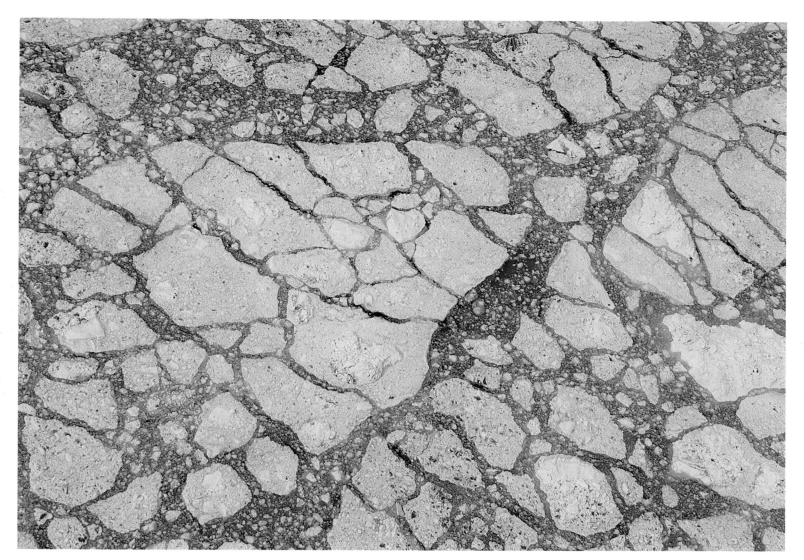

■ *Left:* Icebergs recently calved from McBride Glacier rest on a gravel bar in Muir Inlet, as 5,500-foot Mount Case and 5,139-foot Mount Wright catch the light of the setting sun. ■ *Above:* Extremely active calving by John Hopkins Glacier leaves John Hopkins Inlet choked with pan ice. After a catastrophic retreat over the past two centuries, John Hopkins Glacier is inexorably advancing. The only constant at Glacier Bay seems to be the constant of change itself.

■ *Above:* The high peaks surrounding Glacier Bay collect vast amounts of snow from the Gulf of Alaska's warm, moist air. When accumulation exceeds summer melting, glaciers form. These peaks above Adams Inlet lose most of their snow yearly and consequently do not spawn massive glaciers. ■ *Right:* A cruise ship is dwarfed by seracs of Margerie Glacier. ■ *Following Pages:* Fog graces Nunatak Knob as drizzle falls along the east shore of Muir Inlet.

■ *Above:* In the daily rise and fall of tides, icebergs grind along the shore of Glacier Bay, here silhouetted by reflections of pink cirrus clouds above Tarr Inlet. When floating, five-sixths of an iceberg remains below salt water.
■ *Right:* Lamplugh Glacier, one of about sixteen tidewater glaciers in the park, stands ready to calve more ice into John Hopkins Inlet. The color comes from the ice's tendency to reflect blue light while absorbing other colors.

On a summer day in 1896, a poor placer miner named George Washington Carmack and two Indian companions, Skookum Jim and Tagish Charley, rested at Rabbit Creek, a tributary of the Klondike River, in Canada's Yukon Territory—north of today's Klondike Gold Rush National Historical Park. It is not clear which of the three first saw the gold, but it is certain that this became one of the grandest gold discoveries in North America. Never again would Carmack's life be the same, nor would the lives of thousands of others who flooded north, each convinced fortune was on his side, many of them in store for a rude awakening.

Carmack quickly fashioned a sign: "To Whom It May Concern. I do this day, locate and claim by right of discovery, five hundred feet running upstream from this notice. Located this 17th day of August, 1896. G. W. Carmack."

One year later, he stepped off a steamer in Seattle with a suitcase filled with gold. He and his wife checked into the finest hotel in town, and when his wife, a Native woman, became confused by a labyrinth of halls and doorways, she took her hatchet and blazed a trail on the hotel's beautiful hardwood banister and doorway.

"GOLD. Gold in the Klondike," exclaimed a Seattle newspaper. What better excuse to sail north to the Last Frontier and certain riches. Fields were left half-planted, houses half-built, and businesses half-established. Men who the day before had been considered solid citizens in their communities suddenly packed up and left families, homes, and careers. Some promised to return and did; others promised to return and did not; still others were never heard from again. Hardly any found enough gold to fill a tooth, for by the time the rush began, all the good claims had been staked. But they came anyway, men with dreams in their heads who boarded steamers in Seattle and sailed the Inside Passage of British Columbia and Southeast Alaska eleven hundred miles to the riotous towns of Skagway and Dyea. From there they would hike over the mountains into the Yukon and, they believed, to great riches.

Hardship, friendship, joy, pain, deceit, and death mixed in a great unflowering of youth, where boys became men and men found new lives. Klondike Gold Rush National Historical Park preserves relics of the trek, at Seattle, Skagway, and Dyea, and over the Chilkoot Trail.

Armed with good cheer, three friends and I hiked that trail during three sunny days in July. Tucked into our packs were the poetry of Robert Service and the prose of Jack London and Pierre Berton, each in his own way a child of the Klondike.

Along the Taiya River, past Dyea, Finnegan's Point, Canyon City, Pleasant Camp, and Sheep Camp, past wildflowers, ferns, and towering cottonwoods, the Chilkoot Trail carried us inland—my friends and I—as our footsteps joined those of thousands who had come before. Among them had been a young Jack London who never lost his humor, nor his sanity, and wrote: "The cold, the silence and the darkness somehow seem to be considered the chief woes of the Klondiker. But all this is wrong. There is one woe which overshadows all others—the lack of sugar. Every party which goes north signifies a manly intention to do without sugar and after it gets there bemoans itself upon its lack of foresight. Man can endure hardship and horror with equanimity, but take from him his sugar, and he raises his lamentations to the stars."

From Sheep Camp, the trail climbs steeply toward Chilkoot Pass and the International Boundary. Here, in 1898, the Royal Northwest Mounted Police (now the Royal Canadian Mounted Police) established a customs station requiring every Klondiker to carry a one-year supply of food and clothing into the Yukon. Here men became mules as each made several ascents up to the pass, ferrying up to a hundred pounds of gear on his back.

At the top of Chilkoot Pass, my friends and I stopped to reflect on the history around us—dreams and broken dreams, adventures and misadventures, good men and bad, things that glitter and are not gold—and with the wind at our backs, sugar in our pockets, and good cheer in our hearts, we hiked over the pass and into Canada.

Left: *During the Klondike Gold Rush, thousands of stampeders following the Chilkoot Trail hauled their outfits past this creek cascading toward the Taiya River.* Above: *Hardships were many during the six hundred-mile journey from Skagway and Dyea to Dawson. Many lost their lives, including sixty men in the Palm Sunday 1898 Avalanche near Chilkoot Pass.*

Klondike Gold Rush

■ *Left:* Today, hikers follow the route of the Gold Rush stampeders on the first thirty-three miles of the Chilkoot Trail from tidewater at Dyea to Lake Bennett, British Columbia. Many artifacts from 1898 are spread along the route.
■ *Above:* The Arctic Brotherhood Hall in the Skagway Historic District dates from 1899. Its façade of twenty thousand driftwood sticks was nailed to the front wall in 1900. Skagway boasts over seventy-five Gold Rush-era buildings.

■ *Above:* A rusted saw discarded at Canyon City speaks of a town that flourished but briefly along the Chilkoot Trail. By 1899, a narrow-gauge railroad had been forged through the wilderness to the summit of nearby White Pass. Gold seekers still intent on finding riches in the Great North abandoned the arduous Chilkoot Trail in favor of riding a train. ■ *Right:* Water droplets glisten on fronds of oak fern growing along the Chilkoot Trail.

People called the charming town of Sitka "The Paris of the Pacific" back in the 1840s, when square-rigged sailing ships from around the world filled the harbor and traded their exotic riches. Today, the comparison to Paris is gone, but the charm of Sitka National Historical Park remains. St. Michael's Russian Orthodox Church stands on Lincoln Street, flanked by bookstores, art shops, and eateries. On one side of town is a forest of boat masts in a picturesque harbor; on the other, a forest of spruce and hemlock on steep mountain slopes. Down the road is Sheldon Jackson College, named for the white missionary-educator who pounded Christianity and English into the minds of Tlingits, the Native people of northern Southeast Alaska. And beyond the college, Haida and Tlingit totem poles rise among the trees and speak of proud peoples and proud cultures.

The story here has been told many times—in Tlingit, Russian, and English tongues—for Sitka is a crucible of Alaskan history where cultures clashed and the tides of change washed ashore with unprecedented force. To me, the story pivots on two men, each a charismatic, strong-willed leader of his people, and each determined to thwart the other.

Katlian, a Tlingit of the Kiksadi clan, lashed a blacksmith's hammer to his wrist and pulled a raven helmet over his head to prepare for battle. For centuries his people had lived along the North American coast, developing one of the most sophisticated cultures among Native North Americans. They had made robes and baskets and designed their clan figures—raven, eagle, bear, salmon, killer whale—in characteristic formline design. Life was good until the great white sails arrived.

Aleksandr Baranov, the first chief manager of the Russian-American Company, splashed ashore in 1799. With him were other Russians and Koniag Indians indentured from Kodiak. Alaska was rich with sea otters—"soft gold" Baranov called them—and he needed a base of operations along the Southeast Coast, preferably near the Tlingit village of *Shee Atika*, later mutated by foreign tongues to "Sitka."

Here the coastline provided a protected harbor rich with fish and marine mammals, and a few miles north of present-day Sitka, Baranov and his men built a fort called Redoubt St. Michael. The Tlingits barely tolerated them. Baranov left to attend to business elsewhere, and in 1802, the Tlingits attacked Redoubt St. Michael and killed his men. Some escaped and reported to Baranov in Kodiak.

Retribution was in order. Baranov returned in 1804 with four ships and a full complement of men. Under the leadership of Katlian, the Tlingits armed themselves in a fort outside their village and rebuffed the Russians for six blood-filled days, with both sides using guns and suffering heavy losses. But when Baranov and his men advanced on the seventh day, they found the fort empty. The Tlingits had run out of flints and gunpowder and escaped during the night.

The new stockade and town—the future Sitka—built by Baranov was called New Archangel, and its people set about slaughtering sea otters. Sixty-three years later, in 1867, with otters gone and the Russian-American Company failing, the Russian tsar sold Alaska to the United States for $7.2 million.

Sitka

Today, both the sea otters and the Tlingits have returned. But some of the finest vestiges of Tlingit culture are preserved in Sitka National Historical Park. These include the totem poles along the two miles of quiet pathways (many of them replicas from elsewhere in Southeast Alaska), and the artifacts in the park visitor center. Contemporary artists work in the adjacent Southeast Alaska Indian Cultural Center with the dexterity of their ancestors, perpetuating Tlingit ties with the land and sea, creating images of raven, eagle, killer whale, bear, and salmon—the elements of life in Southeast Alaska.

There is no great monument to Katlian, nor to the entire Tlingit people. It is the victors, not the vanquished, that write history books. The best way to read this story is not in a textbook while seated in a whitewashed room; rather, take a walk down a quiet path at Sitka National Historical Park, pausing to consider what has changed here, and what has not.

Left: *Sitka National Historical Park, established in 1910, commemorates the bloody Battle of Sitka, when Russians attacked the Tlingits in 1804. Above: The Chapel of the Annunciation in the Russian bishop's house holds icons from both Russian settlement and present times. Many Native people of the Russian Orthodox faith worship in nearby St. Michael's Cathedral.*

■ *Left:* Western red cedar is the wood of choice for Haida and Tlingit totem pole carvers. This figure on the Lakich'inei Pole is "the Bear Who Married a Woman." The original carving from Prince of Wales Island was recarved by Native Civilian Conservation Corp members in the 1930s. ■ *Above:* Adapted to temperate rain forest conditions, Sitka spruce, the state tree of Alaska, forms an almost impenetrable barrier near the site of the Battle of Sitka.

■ *Above:* Bishop Innocent, later canonized Saint Innocent, slept in a tiny bed by today's standards. Russian customs of the 1850s called for sleeping with the torso propped up. Common belief was that this would help keep respiratory diseases from settling in the lungs. ■ *Right:* The altar in the Chapel of the Annunciation in the Russian bishop's house has been restored to its 1853 appearance. Russian Orthodox services are still held here occasionally.

The Tlingit Indians called it *Kootznoowoo,* "Fortress of the Bears." In 1794 Captain George Vancouver named it Admiralty Island in honor of the British Navy, the same navy that eighteen years later would sail up the Potomac River and bombard Washington, D.C. Today our maps call it Admiralty Island National Monument, but it is the Tlingit name, *Kootznoowoo,* that comes to mind when you walk a tide flat and discover bear tracks the size of pie plates.

The bear could be miles away, or just inside the forest of Sitka spruce and western hemlock. A loon flaps by. The tide has receded and you kneel to study limpets, mussels, green urchins, and a sunburst starfish. Then, a hundred feet ahead, something moves—a bear, a male Alaskan brown bear to be precise, the world's largest terrestrial carnivore. This is perhaps the most exciting, frightening experience in your life. Stay calm. Do not run. "Bears are dangerous," someone once told you, "but only when threatened, disturbed, or particularly hungry."

How many times before has this bear smelled human scent? He lives on a wilderness island of about seventeen hundred square miles and shares it with roughly seventeen hundred other brown bears (an average of one per square mile) and 650 people. Here is one of the last places in North America where bears outnumber people.

Because you and the bear are at the back of Mitchell Bay, you wonder, "Am I the first person this bear has ever seen?" Rising on his hind feet and waving his nose, he must be nine feet tall. But you remember Mitchell Bay is a popular fishing area for Tlingits from Angoon, the island's only permanent settlement. Certainly this bear has encountered people before. It feels like hours have passed, but it has been only minutes. The tide is rising. Soon your kayak, pulled onto the beach between you and the bear, will float away. Stay calm. The bear finally drops to all four feet, takes one last look at you—strange, two-legged creature of unusual smell and behavior—then turns and walks away.

Bears are not the only story on Admiralty, just the main story. You might also see Sitka black-tailed deer, river otters, or harbor seals. You certainly will see bald eagles, for the shoreline of Admiralty is one of their richest nesting and feeding areas. Shot by bounty hunters for two dollars a bird, an estimated 128,000 were killed from 1917 to 1953 under the assumption that their salmon diet threatened the livelihood of Alaska's commercial fisherfolk. Though bald eagles do eat salmon, they usually eat spawned-out fish as they die in streams and rivers. With legal protection and with the banning of certain pesticides, the eagles have rebounded dramatically, once again adding nobility to the skies of Southeast Alaska.

Moving inland above treeline, the visitor finds spectacular views of Chatham Strait and the Baranof and Chichagof islands to the west and Seymour Canal, Glass Peninsula, Stephens Passage, and the Alaska mainland to the east— if the weather is clear, which is rare. Watch for tide rips, listen for loons, and remember the wisdom of Stan Price.

"The Bear Man at Pack Creek," people called him. He was a simple man, a self-described "hermit" who spoke softly and carried a stick, never a gun, and lived with the bears of Admiralty Island for several decades. His hair was snow-white, his hands rough and calloused. When he first arrived at Pack Creek, on Admiralty's east side, bears were scarce. Hunters had shot most of them and sold their hides. But in time, the bears were protected by law, and the population recovered. Stan himself lived in a cabin on a raft. He knew each bear by name. Only once did he have an altercation with one, when they met on a narrow trail and neither moved aside for the other. The bear batted Stan and broke his shoulder. Aside from that, harmony reigned.

As more people visited Pack Creek in the 1980s and discovered the small white-haired man living there among the bears, a legend began. In 1989, in his nineties, the living legend died. But his legacy—to speak softly and show respect for the bears—will live for a long time. When asked on his deathbed if he had any children, Stan Price replied, "Only my bears."

Left: *The 955,810 acres of Admiralty Island National Monument offer many secluded bays and coves. A rubber Zodiac plies an inlet in Tiedeman Island, which is surrounded by the much larger Admiralty Island.* Above: *A humpback whale exposes its fluke during a feeding dive in Seymour Canal. The waters off Admiralty Island are prime habitat for the humpback.*

■ *Left:* Deposited on high ground by a storm tide, driftwood shelters young Sitka spruce gaining footholds on a rocky shore of Seymour Canal. Nurtured by forty or more inches of rain per year, Admiralty Island supports lush vegetation. ■ *Above:* Sun shining through a shower creates a rainbow beyond the rocky intertidal zone of Tiedeman Island. Vertical layers of black schist contrast with white shell fragments that comprise much of the beach gravel.

■ *Above:* A breaking storm lends mystery to Admiralty Island. Dense forests and bountiful intertidal zones support one Alaskan brown bear per square mile. Each mile of shoreline along Seymour Canal averages at least one bald eagle nest. The wilderness of Admiralty Island National Monument is protected from exploitation by the United States Forest Service. ■ *Right:* Barnacles, mussels, limpets, and other shells decorate a rain-soaked beach.

Though Alaska has its share of misnomers, Misty Fiords National Monument is not one of them. *Misty:* The clouds roll in and settle down. Fog veils the trees, cliffs, inlets, and coves. It can rain all day, all week, darn near all month. "A nice place to live if you're an umbrella," quips a kayaker as water pours off a sou'wester into his spaghetti dinner. About 160 inches of rain fall here each year. *Fiords:* Long tendrils of sea reach inland among conifers and cliffs, embraced in places by gentle contours and forested slopes; in others, by rock-ribbed vaults of granite streaked with ribbonlike waterfalls. *National:* It belongs to us all, not just to timber companies, or fishermen, or the Forest Service, or Alaskans, but to every United States citizen. *Monument:* Let it be. As clearcuts in other areas of Alaska eat away at wilderness only centuries can create, Misty Fiords stands apart as a place where trees are still trees, not timber; where streams still run clean, not silted; where the first sound you hear in the morning is the fluted song of a hermit thrush, not a chainsaw. Here the temperate rain forest stands protected, not cut and milled and shipped away.

Dale Pihlman, a former commercial fisherman, marine biologist, and art instructor, has explored the waters of Misty Fiord for forty years. "My father was a fisherman," he says, "and I remember trolling back in Rudyerd Bay and Walker Cove and Boca de Quadra as a ten-year-old boy, thinking what awesome places they were. Years later I worked for the Alaska Department of Fish and Game and walked streams and counted salmon—it's all given me a sort of paternal feeling for the place."

Dale earned his one hundred-ton passenger vessel captain's license and began operating tour boats from Ketchikan, ferrying people into the more hidden, quiet waters of nearby Misty Fiords. He keeps a log of his passengers' comments, a sampling of which reads: "I felt as though I were in another world . . ." "Magnificent scenery, wish I could have stayed a week rather than a day . . ." "Beautiful and free of obvious commercialization . . ." "Wondrous solitude . . ." "Porpoises, seals, mountain goats, bears, hallelujah . . ." "A tremendous blending of mountains and water; beautiful beyond imagination . . ."

The rock walls of Rudyerd Bay and Walker Cove climb three thousand feet above the sea, reminiscent, in a sense, of a coastal, rain forest version of California's Yosemite Valley.

Gentle slopes below the cliffs support Sitka spruce, western hemlock, and western red cedar, some of the grand old trees reaching two hundred feet high. In itself, this forest is a magical place. Step into it, and sounds become muted, the light dims. Mosses and lichens carpet the floor and hang like beards from the branches. Every nook and furrow is a different shade of green—apple, beryl, emerald, jade, olive, and shamrock—and even the air itself seems green. If hobbits and elves truly did exist, they would be here. And wizards, too.

Hike to a lake—Grace, Nooya, Humpback, Manzanita, Winstanley, Lower Ella, Lower Checats, or to the best of them all, Punchbowl Lake—and Misty Fiords will show a new face at every turn in the trail. Glaciers carved cliffs and excavated lakes and fjords, and some glaciers still exist in the monument's northern corners. But volcanoes have a story here, too. New Eddystone Rock, a remnant plug from an old volcano, was so named by Captain George Vancouver in 1794 because it reminded him of Eddystone Lighthouse in Plymouth, England.

Beyond landscape and sheer beauty, Misty Fiords is an ecological bank that provides important habitat for many organisms. All five species of northeastern Pacific salmon spawn here, and for the king salmon—the largest of them all—nearly half its Southeast Alaska spawning and rearing grounds are in Misty Fiords.

I asked monument ranger Paul Brewster what his strongest feelings were about this place. He told me Misty Fiords is the second-largest wilderness in the Forest Service System—an important element—and one of only three national monuments managed by the U.S. Forest Service. The other two are Admiralty Island and Mount St. Helens. And his feelings? "Well," he said, "I think I am one of the luckiest people in the world to be able to work here."

Left: *Misty Fiords is one of the wettest places in North America, receiving an average of 160 inches of liquid precipitation annually. Fog lingering along granite mountains and over icy water lends a mystical appearance to Punchbowl Lake.* Above: *Soon after the winter snow has melted, the sheathed spadices of yellow skunk cabbage decorate poorly drained areas.*

■ *Left:* Boulders and the narrow base of a sea stack are exposed by low tide at Checats Cove in the Behm Canal. The rocks are glacial erratics left by great rivers of ice that gouged and scoured deep fjords during the last Ice Age.
■ *Above:* Numerous waterfalls drop down a sheer granite face to Punchbowl Lake. Much of Misty Fiords resembles Yosemite National Park, except that here the valley floors are filled with crystalline lakes or with sparkling saltwater.

■ *Above:* A stunted forest of lodgepole pine grows from wet, acidic, peaty soils interlaced with shallow ponds. Beyond are granite mountains cradling Little and Big Goat lakes. ■ *Right:* Thick moss embraces branches of a cedar snag along Behm Canal at Edith Point. From sea level to timberline at 2,500 to 3,000 feet, a luxuriant forest of Sitka spruce, western hemlock, western red cedar and Alaska cedar clothes all but rocky cliffs and poorly drained muskeg.

The powerful heart of Katmai National Park and Preserve beats inside those things that embody it: volcanoes and bears. Living, steaming volcanoes are here, as well as approximately eight hundred Alaska brown bears, the largest protected population in the state. Spend a week in Katmai listening to the land, water, wind, and wildlife, and you begin to believe wilderness has a chance.

The park can be divided into three geographic provinces: lake, mountain, and coast. On the coast, where relatively few people go, bears dig for clams, and commercial fisherfolk anchor their boats, both waiting for salmon. Puffins, guillemots, cormorants, and bald eagles are common, as well as sea otters and sea lions, though probably not as common as before May 1989 when oil from the *Exxon Valdez* fouled a major portion of the Katmai Coast. Shelikof Strait, lying between the coast and Kodiak Island, thirty miles to the east, has been called "the roughest stretch of water in Alaska." Things get wild out there. Although good landfall sites and protected anchorages are rare, grand scenery is not. From sea cliffs to islets to tide flats to sandy beaches, the Katmai Coast has it all.

Most visitors head for Brooks Camp, on the shore of Naknek Lake, west of the Aleutian Range, where people, planes, boats, bears, and fish all manage to squeeze into the same place at the same time, creating a wilderness version of Grand Central Station. Come July when the sockeye salmon run, bears gather at Brooks Falls to fish as their mothers taught them, some standing in deep water pools, others along the shore, and others atop the falls, all to the amazement of visitors watching from a nearby "bear-viewing platform."

Other fishermen—the two-legged variety—also try their luck and skill in the Brooks River. They arrive from distant places, pull on chest waders and fishing vests and hats covered with hand-tied flies, and wade into the river downstream from the falls. They catch trout and salmon and speak in accents suspiciously Texan and German. They catch their fish, release many of them as if it were a game, and retire back to Brooks Lodge to tell tall tales and watch the evening sunlight paint amber light over the slopes of Mount Katolinat.

With so many bears and people in the same place, some observers think Brooks Camp is an accident waiting to happen. George Stroud, a former longtime ranger at Katmai, once took a five-day kayak trip on what is called the Savonoski Loop. Leaving Brooks Camp, he paddled through the Bay of Islands on Naknek Lake, portaged across to Lake Grosvenor, headed southeast toward the mountains and then floated down the Savonoski River back to Naknek Lake, a total of seventy-five miles. "After five days out there with the peace and quiet," he said, "Brooks Camp was like a circus."

No trip to Katmai would be complete without going to Brooks Camp, nor would it be complete by going *only* to Brooks Camp. Lakes, like precious jewels, spread to the north—Grosvenor, Coville, Nonvianuk, Kulik, and Battle— each flanked by the Aleutian Mountains to the east and rolling hills to the west, and each with a lodge or a cluster of cabins nestled on its shore next to a river. Here, loons call across the evening water, and moose and bears track the shore. Some nights are windless; most are not. But every night surrenders to a new morning when light like a symphony plays across the patterns of forest, tundra, and water.

Between the lakes and the coast stands the Aleutian Range, an igneous and sedimentary backbone mantled in ice and snow with summits bearing the names Martin, Megeik, Katmai, Trident, and Kukak, to name a few. They are a temperamental bunch, these mountains, sometimes steaming, always alive, for they belong to the Pacific Rim of Fire, having arisen through the grand geological processes called plate tectonics and continental drift. More than a dozen active volcanoes are here, any of which could suddenly blow its top, destroying and creating grand landscapes on a scale and speed fittingly Alaskan.

Take the Valley of Ten Thousand Smokes. For a long time, perhaps centuries, people traveled a trade route between Bristol Bay and Shelikof Strait, journeying through what was

Katmai

Left: *The River Lethe cuts through soft deposits of welded ash and tuff in the Valley of Ten Thousand Smokes. Novarupta's 1912 eruption drained the magma body beneath nearby Mount Katmai, causing its collapse. The explosion was heard seven hundred miles away in Juneau.* Above: *A brown bear sow guards her cubs as they observe fishing at Brooks Falls.*

then a forested valley in the shadow of a mountain called Katmai. By foot, sled, and bidarka—over land, river, and sea—they made the epic journey, stopping along the way at Pawik (Naknek) and Savonoski villages. Then, in early June 1912, the region around Katmai began to rumble. Other mountains steamed nearby, and on June 6 came the big bang: an explosion heard seven hundred miles away in Juneau and since estimated to have been ten times more powerful than the 1980 eruption of Mount St. Helens. The upper two thousand feet of Mount Katmai collapsed, flares swept across the sky such that "the mountains were like sunshine," and the forested valley was buried hundreds of feet deep in a river of volcanic ash.

"My Dear Wife Tania:" wrote a fisherman from Kaflia Bay, on the coast due east of the erupting volcano. "First of all I will let you know of our unlucky voyage. I do not know whether we shall be either alive or well. A mountain has burst near here, so that we are covered with ashes, in some places 10 feet and 6 feet deep. All this began the 6th of June. Night and day we lit lamps. We cannot see the daylight. In a word, it is terrible, and we are expecting death at any moment, and we have no water. All the rivers are covered with ashes. Just ashes mixed with water. Here are darkness and hell, thunder and noise. I do not know whether it is day or night. Vanka will tell you about it. So kissing you and blessing you both, good-bye. Forgive me. Perhaps we shall see each other again. God is merciful. Pray for us. Your husband, Ivan Orloff." He survived.

Five years later, a National Geographic Society expedition ascended Katmai Pass from Shelikof Strait. Robert F. Griggs, leader of the expedition, wrote, "The sight that flashed into view as we surmounted the hillock was one of the most amazing visions ever beheld by mortal eye. The whole valley as far as the eye could reach was full of hundreds, no thousands—literally tens of thousands—of smokes curling up from its fissured floor. From our position they looked as small as the little fumaroles near by, but realizing something of their distance we knew many of them must be gigantic. Some were sending up columns of steam which rose a thousand feet before dissolving."

Unable to sleep that night, Griggs resolved that if ever there was a spectacle worth protecting, this was it. Two years later, in 1918, President Woodrow Wilson exercised powers derived from the 1906 Antiquities Act and established Katmai National Monument.

Nearly all of the smokes are gone today, and the valley, now called the Valley of Ten Thousand Smokes, is no longer forested or a trade route but one of the most unusual landscapes in Alaska. Go out there. The wind might knock you off your feet. Ash might billow up and fill your eyes. The River Lethe might sweep you away and drown you. It has happened before. Or you might kneel before a Kamchatka rhododendron in a still prism of evening air, watch sunset fill the valley with cinnabar light, or stand beside the volcanic plug called Novarupta where the great explosion of 1912 occurred, causing the collapse of Mount Katmai about five miles away. You might make your entry in the log book at the Baked Mountain Cabin, as others have before you:

"Toto, I don't think we're in Kansas anymore." "Hiked over the pass from Katmai Bay. Glad to have done it, but will never do it again." "Sunset is now a rich orange. Clouds look like some of the rocks I've seen. We're alone tonite at the cabin. So wonderfully lonely! God gave us this day."

God gave us this land, too. And everything in it. He gave us the choice to preserve it with wisdom or to plunder it with greed. Thus far, wisdom has prevailed. A park has been born. People from around the world have arrived to watch bears catch fish, to walk in a volcanic valley, and to hear loons call. There have been setbacks: Katmai Coast, now sullied with oil, will not be the same for a long time. But there have been victories as well. Each offers lessons that speak to the importance of wild places like Katmai; lessons that simply say: here is the last, best hope for pristine wilderness in the United States. What are you going to do with it?

Above: *Bears are not the only ones competing for salmon in the Brooks River. An angler wets a fly while watching for* Ursus arctos. Right: *When red salmon run in mid-July, brown bears stake out prime fishing spots at Brooks Falls.* Following Pages: *Almost eighty years after the cataclysmic eruption of Novarupta, fireweed reappears in the Valley of Ten Thousand Smokes.*

■ *Left:* Volcanic fury and roaming brown bears are only part of the Katmai story. There are peaceful elements as well. Mount Katolinat is serenely reflected in a pond along the shore of Iliuk Arm of Naknek Lake. ■ *Above:* Viewed from the air, caribou of the Alaska Peninsula Herd walk single file through a dense clump of alders near Takayoto Creek. To avoid insects in early summer, caribou often congregate in dense groups on the windswept ridges.

■ *Above:* When Novarupta blew, nearby limestone and shale mountains at the crest of the Aleutian Range were scoured and baked by clouds of volcanic ash traveling at speeds greater than one hundred miles an hour. Cool now, the summit of Mount Cerberus rises from a bed of volcanic ash. ■ *Right:* One of fifteen active volcanoes in the park, 6,050-foot Mount Martin rises into the clouds. One certainty at Katmai is the inevitability of future volcanic eruptions.

Father Bernard Hubbard was no ordinary Catholic priest. A Jesuit, he seemed a blend of St. Francis of Assisi, Huck Finn, and Roald Amundsen, dashing across Alaska sixty years ago in search of the most outlandish corners of America's Last Frontier. With Blue-eyed Megeik in the lead, he mushed his dogs down the frozen Yukon River to the Bering Sea and from there traveled along the Alaska Peninsula to Katmai's Valley of Ten Thousand Smokes, then south to Shishaldin Volcano, Bogoslof Island, and finally, in 1930, to "truly a hell on earth" and his "greatest adventure," what is now Aniakchak National Monument and Preserve.

Once a mighty seven-thousand-foot mountain on the Alaska Peninsula, Aniakchak is what remains after ancient eruptions, or perhaps one cataclysmic explosion, destroyed the entire top of that mountain, blasting off an estimated fifteen cubic miles of rock and ash. In the paths of destruction, however, lay the seeds of creation, in this case a caldera six miles across from rim to rim, painted with volcanics, patterned by snow, contoured by cinder cones and anointed with a lake. Most remarkable, however, was the abundance of life.

"The first sight of Aniakchak takes your breath away," exclaimed Father Hubbard when he flew into the caldera with a bush pilot and landed on Surprise Lake. "It is too big to comprehend in a few moments." Out of the plane jumped Blue-eyed Megeik and the other dogs. A few days later Hubbard was joined by his companions who hiked into Aniakchak from the coast. Exploring the steaming fumaroles and hot rocks, Hubbard exclaimed, "If Virgil, Homer and Dante had seen anything like this, they really would have had something to write about." What astounded Hubbard most, though, were the salmon in the lake, the bear tracks in the ash, the hidden nests of ptarmigan, the fox den on a lava hill. "The more we observed, the more fully we were convinced that Aniakchak was a world complete in itself . . . a world inside a mountain." Hubbard called it "Paradise Found."

That next year, in 1931, Aniakchak erupted and Father Hubbard wasted little time returning. "Climbing to the crater rim," he wrote in *National Geographic* magazine, "we were going through a valley of death in which not a blade of grass or a flower or a bunch of moss broke through the thick covering of deposited ash. . . . Several hours of hard work, and but a few feet separated us from the coveted goal, the rim of Aniakchak, and the first glance into the great abyss. . . . Kneeling, as is our custom on such occasions, we said our 'Hail Mary' aloud; then crawled cautiously to the edge. Silence. Nobody wanted to speak. There was the new Aniakchak, but it was the abomination of desolation, it was the prelude of hell. Black walls, black floor, black water, deep black holes and black vents. . . . No longer did the beautifully colored lavas and shiny volcanic glass strike the vision. No streams coursed through flower-strewn meadows, no grassy slopes led up to former volcanic vents; no glistening glaciers or snowfields broke the monotony of the huge crater walls. . . . Beautiful Surprise Lake . . . was choked and muddy and black. . . . We stood awestricken on the edge, looking, like Dante, into a real inferno." Paradise Found had become Paradise Lost.

And so the pendulum swings—nature creates, nature destroys. Since 1931, nature's pendulum has made significant progress. The fields of lava and ash remain, but brightening them are green meadows and the reds, purples, and yellows of more than seventy species of wildflowers. Surprise Lake is indeed a surprise, for among its residents are algae, invertebrates, Dolly Varden char, and sockeye salmon. As new plant communities establish themselves, new habitats arise. Brown bears, caribou, wolverines, porcupines, weasels, red fox, an occasional wolf, and about forty species of birds have found their way here.

Caldera and coast both fit into Aniakchak National Monument and Preserve, 425 miles down the Alaska Peninsula from Anchorage. The wind can blow one hundred miles an hour, and the rain can fall for days on end, but when the storm breaks and the sky opens above the "world within a mountain," perhaps even Father Hubbard would be lost for words.

Aniakchak

Left: *Beyond volcanic bombs polished by wind-blown cinders, clouds spill over the rim of Aniakchak Caldera. Renowned for fierce storms with one hundred-mile winds, Aniakchak is the least-visited national monument open to the public.* Above: *Volcanic basalt and pumice decorate Vent Mountain's slope. The 3,350-foot peak is really a volcano within a volcano.*

■ *Left:* A small spatter cone shimmers in the glassy water of Surprise Lake. Stretching over two miles, this is the remnant of a much larger caldera-filling lake that drained when the caldera wall was broken by the Aniakchak River.

■ *Above:* The last eruption of Aniakchak, in 1931, obliterated life within the crater. Since then, plants have regained a tenuous hold. Blasted by wind-blown cinders, narrow strips of bark bring sustenance to green willow leaves.

■ *Above:* Life abounds in the desolate landscape comprising the thirty-square-mile caldera. To the slightly turbid waters of Surprise Lake migrate annually sockeye salmon and fish-hungry brown bears. Over 138 identified vascular plant species grow on volcanic soils. ■ *Right:* Warm springs, lacking oxygen but rich in iron, precipitate iron oxides when the water mingles with air. Thermal activity quietly speaks of far greater volcanic power lurking below.

In the 1970s, when a task force of the National Park Service came looking for an exemplary piece of Alaska's coast—a place with headlands and mudflats, inlets and icefields, pounding surf and glass-smooth coves, glaciers and guillemots, sea lions and starfish, conifers and otters—they found Kenai Fjords. Ten years later, when Stan Carrick and I wanted to try our hand at sea kayaking in a double Klepper, we also found Kenai Fjords National Park.

When we ended up paddling for our lives in gale-force winds and six-foot seas—"Stan, we're in trouble, turn to starboard"—we happened into a nameless cove in Yalik Bay, surfed onto shore with the wind at our backs, staggered into the forest, pitched our tent, and fell asleep on a wet bed of moss in the pouring rain. "Camping doesn't get more miserable than this," Stan mumbled as he placed a tin cup beneath a leak in the tent. For four days and four nights the rain came down. We peered outside for Noah, but he wasn't around, nor were his animals.

Go through an experience like that and you will not forget the first morning that dawns bright and clear. Sunlight melts the air. Droplets of rain hang like prisms from spruce needles and shine like diamonds in the leaflets of lupine. Thrushes and kinglets sing. Bald eagles call.

Stan and I stepped out of the tent and basked in the warmth. Yalik Bay lapped gently at the shore. We hung our clothes to dry and an hour later climbed in the kayak to paddle around lazily and look at the mountains, forests, and sea. I remember not saying much, just slipping into silence, then letting Kenai Fjords do the talking. Water trickled against the Klepper, a harbor seal splashed, sea ducks spoke in dialects of harlequin, goldeneye, and scaup. Then the floatplane arrived, and we disassembled the Klepper and bid farewell to the thrushes and kinglets.

"The Alaska coast is to become the showplace of the earth, and pilgrims, not only from the United States, but from beyond the seas, will throng in endless processions to see it," wrote the preeminent geographer Henry Gannett after sailing off the southern coast of the Kenai Peninsula (and into Glacier Bay, Prince William Sound, and elsewhere) as a member of the Harriman Alaska Expedition of 1899. "There is one other asset of the Territory not yet enumerated, imponderable, and difficult to appraise, yet one of the chief assets of Alaska, if not the greatest," he continued. "This is the scenery. . . . Its grandeur is more valuable than the gold or the fish or the timber, for it will never be exhausted. . . . If you are old, go by all means; but if you are young, wait. The scenery of Alaska is much grander than anything else of the kind in the world, and it is not well to dull one's capacity for enjoyment by seeing the finest first."

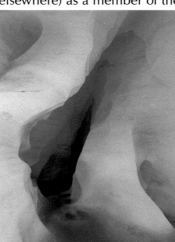

My wife, Melanie, and I first visited Kenai Fjords many years ago as passengers on a tour boat based in Seward. We were thirty something—not so young, not so old—and fully prepared to dull our capacity for enjoyment. This was several years before my kayak trip with Stan Carrick. The morning dawned clear and calm. Sea otters swam in the harbor, and eagles perched on the pilings—otters and eagles that someday would be imperiled, perhaps killed, by the *Exxon Valdez* oil spill. The town bustled with a new sawmill.

We traveled down Resurrection Bay and around Callisto Head until Bear Glacier came into view in full sunshine. Near Agnes Cove we spotted two humpback whales, a mother and calf. The captain kept his distance, but the whales approached and surfaced only one hundred feet away. For ten minutes, though it seemed like an hour, they lingered nearby before finally raising their flukes and diving deep. Around Aialik Cape, past Three Hole Point and across Aialik Bay to Holgate Glacier, we sat on the bow feasting on peanuts, chocolate, and magnificent scenery. Euphoria crept over us, induced by the sights and sounds of Kenai Fjords. The captain shut down the engine, and we drifted a quarter mile off the tidewater face of Holgate Glacier, staring into the crystalline blue walls of the Ice Age.

Left: *Only the tallest mountain peaks, called nunataks, break the white expanse of the Harding Icefield, which covers nearly three hundred square miles with ice up to a mile thick. Above: An ice cave in a glacier toe on the south shore of Holgate Arm invites exploration. However, falling ice and a deep entrance pool keep its chambers unvisited.*

"That glacier flows out of the Harding Icefield just like a river flows out of a lake," the captain told us. To hear about the Harding is one thing, to see it is another, for not just one sea borders Kenai Fjords, but two—one of water, the other of ice. From the boat I could only visualize how the icefield must look and I carried those visions with me until Stan Carrick and I flew over the top, homeward bound, and saw the real thing. Below us lay three hundred square miles of ice broken occasionally by serrated, nameless peaks like islands amid a Pleistocene ocean. Here glaciers are born, I thought to myself, glaciers that carved the coastline we see today and have since retreated from areas reclaimed by the sea: Aialik Bay, Harris Bay, Northwestern Lagoon, McCarty Fjord, Nuka Bay. Where ice once reigned, life now flourishes with alpine meadows, mountain goats, forests, moose, tide pools, otters, salmon streams, eagles, plankton, and whales.

Glaciers have budgets balanced between income and expenditure. Income is the rate of snow accumulation and ice creation at higher elevations, in this case the Harding Icefield. Expenditure is the rate of ice melting and calving at lower elevations (calving being the process of ice falling off the glacier's tidewater terminus into the sea). At equilibrium, when neither exceeds the other, a glacial terminus remains stationary. Should snowfall increase over a period of many years, a glacial terminus will likely advance. Should snowfall decrease, however, a glacial terminus will likely retreat. This does not mean a glacier flows upslope or backwards. Glaciers by definition always flow downslope and forwards. They are rivers of H_2O in a solid rather than liquid state. Only the terminus of a glacier retreats, like a conveyor belt moving downhill, growing shorter as its lower end disappears.

In Kenai Fjords, as in almost every other piece of Alaska's glaciated maritime coast, the balance has been tipped recently with expenditures exceeding income. Underfed and over-extended, the glaciers have retreated and opened fjords to the sea. Now add to this scenario the process called plate tectonics, author of the Good Friday Earthquake of 1964—the strongest quake recorded in North America—which sank the coast of Kenai Fjords six feet in a matter of minutes. Two of the earth's great crustal plates meet here, each dragging the other downward. The entire southern flank of the Kenai Peninsula is sinking while the northern end rises like the opposite end of a seasaw. Areas that millennia ago were alpine valleys now lie beneath the sea off the Southcentral Coast of Alaska.

The return trip was not so smooth. A strong wind kicked up, sloshing us around the seabird and sea lion colonies on the Chiswell Islands, part of the Alaska Maritime National Wildlife Refuge. We then turned up Resurrection Bay and practically surfed back to Seward on huge six-foot waves. Former National Park Service photographer M. Woodbridge Williams once described this area through the words of others: "Paradise Cove, Beauty Bay, Beautiful Island, Surprise Bay, and Delight Lake. These names reflected the impressions made on early explorers by the inside waters of Alaska's Kenai Fjords. Their impressions sang another song: Wildcat Pass, Thunder Bay, Cloudy Cape, and Roaring Cove."

Roaring is right. By nightfall a storm had moved in and Kenai Fjords was awash with wind and rain, the kind of weather Stan Carrick and I would encounter at the southern end of the park in Yalik Bay. When it rains down low, it snows up high on the Harding Icefield—several feet at a time, in fact, and thirty-five to sixty-five feet per year. This is the stuff of glaciers, the architects of Kenai Fjords National Park.

The great ice rivers have ebbed before and flowed back, and every time I refer to the Ice Age in the past tense, I catch myself, for if the fjords could speak and we could listen, I believe they would say the past is the key to the future, and what has happened before will happen again: glaciers will advance, glaciers will retreat, and the coast will be sculpted anew. For now, though, as whales, otters, and eagles enrich the area, and sawmills, oil spills, and cheap thrills threaten it, I wonder if ever again life will be the same in Kenai Fjords.

Above: Two horned puffins are among the thousands of birds that nest on cliffs and islands at Kenai Fjords National Park. *Right:* Deep crevasses dissect a glacier spilling off the Harding Icefield toward McCarty Fjord. The icefield spawns thirty glaciers, eight of which reach tidewater. *Following Pages:* Icebergs line the shore of a lake adjacent to Pederson Glacier.

■ *Left:* A tour boat pauses at Three Hole Point, a popular destination in Aialik Bay. Carved by wave action, the sea arches have many cracks that provide secure homes for honed puffins. ■ *Above:* From a stark habitat of limestone cobbles tossed on the shore of Bulldog Cove grow salmonberry and dwarf fireweed. Generally, only the greatest of spring and autumn tides, as well as severe winter storms, inundate these highest beaches with saltwater.

■ *Above:* The Good Friday Earthquake of 1964 lowered the coast of Kenai Fjords by six feet. Shoreline spruce, as in Bear Cove of Aialik Bay, were killed by saltwater flooding. Their skeletons bear mute testimony to the powers of plate tectonics. ■ *Right:* The Gulf of Alaska laps at Black Mountain. The Kenai Fjords Coast resembles a mountain range being sucked beneath the sea. Subduction of the North American plate swallows the Kenai Mountains.

The saying that Lake Clark National Park and Preserve epitomizes Alaska persists because it is true. "Think of all the splendors that bespeak Alaska," wrote John Kauffmann in *Exploring America's Backcountry,* "glaciers, volcanoes, alpine spires, wild rivers, lakes with grayling on the rise. Picture coasts feathered with countless seabirds. Imagine dense forests and far-sweeping tundra, herds of caribou, great roving bears. Now concentrate all these and more into less than one percent of the state—and behold the Lake Clark region, Alaska's epitome." And only an hour from Anchorage by small plane.

"It's like flying into the mouth of a shark," the pilot said the first time I flew through Lake Clark Pass. Mountains like teeth loomed off each wingtip. Blue sky opened above, glaciated land spread below. Turbulence rocked the small plane like a toy. "It can get a lot worse than this," the pilot barked. "Great," I groaned. But the turbulence quieted down, so did the pilot, and we flew up the Kijik River and over Twin Lakes before doubling back above patterns, textures, and colors of tundra, taiga, mountain, and lake to land at Port Alsworth on Lake Clark.

The scenery had silenced us, but a voice whispered inside me: this is Richard Proenneke's country. I had heard of this man for years but never met him and still have not, which is my loss. People in the area call him Dick, and though many of those people are equally friendly and fascinating—the Alsworths, Hammonds, Twitchells, Bowmans, and others—no story of Lake Clark would be complete without Dick Proenneke, a bacon and sourdough hotcake man who works with his hands and rises with the sun to greet what he calls, "the awakening land."

Carpenter, diesel mechanic, heavy equipment operator, commercial fisherman, Proenneke earned his pay in the greasy sleeve corners of Alaska for seventeen years before a friend invited him on a trip over the mountains to Lake Clark country. Something about wilderness had always appealed to him, and here was country finer than any he had ever imagined. Time was marching on, it was 1967, and Proenneke was fifty. He quit his job, traveled to Iowa to visit his family, and that next spring returned to Anchorage, climbed into a Cessna 180 with Babe Alsworth and flew to Lake Clark.

A few days later they continued to Twin Lakes, north of Lake Clark and seventeen hundred feet higher. And there, in 1968, while civil rights and assassinations rocked the rest of America, Dick Proenneke quietly built a humble, elegant cabin amid the spruce, mountains, and lapping shore of Twin Lakes. "It was good to be back in the wilderness again where everything seems at peace," he wrote. "It was a great feeling . . . a stirring feeling." "May 30th . . . A trace of new snow on the crags." "June 28th . . . Bright as crystal this morning and not a cloud to be seen." "July 8th . . . The weather changes like a man's fortunes." "August 12th . . . The spruce boughs are glistening with rain drops. The land had a bath last night." "September 18th . . . Foggy and calm. Twenty-two degrees." "November 28th . . . Thanksgiving day. Clear, calm and a minus four degrees. The stars still out at eight o'clock this morning. The lake is white with frost. . . ."

Twenty-three years later, Dick Proenneke, seventy-four, still lives alone in his cabin amid the spruce and mountains of Twin Lakes. His home is an enclave now in a young national park, and from the busy streets of Anchorage I can see the rugged Chigmit Mountains that guard his world from mine. May it forever remain that way.

The Chigmits form a rugged barrier. John Kauffmann wrote, "To some, they are Alaska's Alps, so tight and deep a mountain maze that each portion is a private world. Only the doughtiest trekkers have crossed the Chigmits on foot, braving flood and thicket and crevasse."

Among them is former park ranger Fred Hirschmann. Together with another ranger he hiked from the coast to Kontrashibuna Lake in an ordeal he says he will never forget. Beginning at Tuxedni Bay, he and his partner followed the Tuxedni River and moved upslope through thickets of devil's club and alder. In one ten-hour period of hiking—better described as alder-bashing—they covered only two and a quarter miles. Not exactly a country stroll. But the worst

Left: *Yellow willows and red dwarf birch join a pair of white spruce standing sentinel along the shore of Lower Twin Lake.* Above: *Kathleen Trefon laughs from the entrance of her grandfather's wall tent on the shore of Lake Clark. Each fall, the Dena'ina family leaves the village of Nondalton and travels uplake to secure a winter supply of berries and salmon.*

Lake Clark

was yet to come. About the time they reached the crest of the Chigmits, so did a storm. Fred remembers, "We camped by a small lake, and the howling wind sheared water off the lake and slammed the spray against nearby mountains. Both tent poles snapped, so we sat inside for twenty straight hours and braced the poles with our arms, using duct tape and an old C-rations can to hold the poles together at the top. Twenty-seven boulders and two ice axes held the tent down!" The storm subsided, and they hiked into Gladiator Basin where thick fog confused their senses of direction and distance. "I saw a bull moose that looked far away," says Hirschmann, "but after taking a few more steps I realized he was too near for comfort." Eventually, Fred and his partner made their way to Port Alsworth, field headquarters of the park. The twenty-eight-mile trip had taken them eight days.

Most hikers head for the lake country, northwest of the Chigmits, where walking is easier on high, dry tundra, and Lake Clark National Park abuts against Lake Clark National Preserve. Here the headwaters of the Telaquana, Mulchatna, and Chilikadrotna rivers tumble like their names out the southern end of the Alaska Range and into picturesque lakes—Telaquana, Turquoise, and Twin—before continuing west and south to Bristol Bay. Moose feed in willow thickets, Dall sheep dwell on mountain slopes, and the Mulchatna caribou herd migrates to and from normal summer calving grounds in the Turquoise-Telaquana-Twin lakes region.

In a way, lakes are a crucible in this park, as perhaps they should be since Lake Clark itself is the centerpiece. On calm evenings, the mountains are reflected with breathtaking clarity in the glassy waters; yet on wild, windy days the lakes grow angry with whitecaps, and storms can capsize canoes, kayaks, and even small planes. But perhaps the greatest story about these lakes and rivers belongs not above the water, but below—to the sockeye salmon.

All five species of Pacific salmon migrate into the park, but none as much as the sockeye. Part of the reason for creating Lake Clark National Park, in fact, was to help protect the sockeye. Every July, they surge by the millions into Bristol Bay and up the Togiak, Nushagak, Kvichak, Naknek, Egegik and Ugashik rivers, bound for spawning grounds from whence they came. The Kvichak has been called the "world's finest spawning ground for sockeye." In one ten-year period, this system supplied 55 percent of the Bristol Bay catch, 33 percent of the U.S. catch,

and 16 percent of the world catch. This despite the fact that of the approximately three thousand eggs each female lays, the odds are that fewer than thirty will survive to adulthood, and of those thirty perhaps only one or two will survive to spawn. Larger fish eat the salmon in their youth; marine mammals eat them in their later years; frantic commercial fisherfolk catch them by the hundreds of thousands in the July waters of Bristol Bay.

Greed plays its part here; though the fishery is strictly regulated, the scene nevertheless has disturbing overtones of a century or two ago when Alaska's coast was a sea of slaughter and furriers needed only a few years to decimate otters and seals in Tuxedni and Chinitna bays. Also devastated were the native Dena'ina Indians of Lake Clark, killed not only by guns and knives but by measles, smallpox, and influenza— white man's diseases. The historical village of Kijik was abandoned, and most members of the six remaining families eventually resettled at Nondalton, on Six Mile Lake below Lake Clark.

Populations have stabilized since those destructive times. The fish and wildlife are closely watched, and the Dena'ina stoically accept their crossroads between the old world and new as a culture and a corporation.

Nature never lies down out here and never will. Wind blows cold and strong over the lakes, salmon and caribou follow ancient migration routes, and the great volcanoes at the top of the Chigmit Mountains—Iliamna and Redoubt—decide every thirty years or so to erupt.

From Anchorage I see a plume of ash and steam over Redoubt's summit right now. Some think it will blow its top, but I think of Dick Proenneke instead, the bacon and sourdough hotcake man, living his solitary life and rising with the sun to greet "the awakening land."

Above: Moss campion on the slope of the Chigmit Mountains is only one of an estimated one thousand species of plants that eventually are expected to be found within the borders of Lake Clark National Park and Preserve. *Right:* Beyond a tidal slough slicing across the mudflats of Cook Inlet looms the peak of volcanic 10,016-foot Mount Iliamna.

■ *Left:* The Tusk, a glacially carved monolith, rises seventeen hundred feet. A highlight of flights through Merrill Pass, few people have visited the Tusk via foot. Four attempts at climbing the friable granite spire have been made. Only one succeeded. ■ *Above:* Leaves of alpine bearberry add a spot of scarlet to the tundra along the Stony River. ■ *Following Pages:* Crisp September mornings bring fog lifting off Lower Twin Lake and reveal brilliant autumn color.

■ *Above:* Plummage of a male willow ptarmigan blends with the warm brown tones of autumn willow leaves. A few white feathers foretell the coming moult that will turn the ptarmigan as white as the winter snows. ■ *Right:* Summer passes into winter with but a brief interlude known as fall. Through September, each day has six to nine minutes less sunlight than the day before. An intricate pattern of ice forms on the surface of a small pool as freeze-up begins.

■ *Left:* A lone fireweed turns brilliant red on a rocky bed of spruce needles above Portage Lake. Fireweed's name comes not from the color of its fall foliage but from its propensity to pioneer disturbed soils, especially following forest fires. ■ *Above:* Of the scores of spectacular waterfalls in Lake Clark National Park and Preserve, only Tanalian Falls bears an official name. Two miles of trail lead from the community of Port Alsworth to the falls.

The Inupiat Eskimos say, "Only the wind knows the way of the caribou." Perhaps then, here in Kobuk Valley National Park, above the Arctic Circle on the southwest flank of the Brooks Range, only the caribou know the way of the Kobuk, for they have occupied this land for a long time, and so have the Eskimos. Encircled by the Baird, Schwatka, and Jade mountains is a broad valley with a river running through it. Both are called Kobuk.

Here, subarctic meets arctic, boreal forest meets tundra, Beringia becomes America and sand dunes rise in smooth counterpoint to the surrounding land. Here, if time were a window, we would see the hunters of a hundred generations who lived and died in this remote corner of our continent. They hunted caribou, fished for salmon and sheefish, and left their tools in the cold earth where, thousands of years later, archaeologists found them. At Onion Portage, a shelf above a river bend where caribou traditionally cross the Kobuk, J. Louis Giddings began a series of investigations that would culminate in the discovery of what has been hailed by the Smithsonian Institution as the "most significant archaeological site ever found in the Arctic." Historian William Brown added that Onion Portage, together with the successive beach ridges at Cape Krusenstern, provide "the benchmarks of Arctic archaeology."

What exultation Giddings must have felt upon discovering this place where Eskimos gathered for generations, hunting caribou and sharing stories, leaving their tools like calling cards above the banks of the ancient Kobuk. "Somewhat incredulous," he wrote in 1961, "I sank a limited test cut and found to my elation that there was no limit to the neatly stacked layering of old surfaces. Furthermore, the differences in nature and style of the flinty material in one after another of these charcoal-bearing layers showed that they were not simply the occupation zones of closely successive visitors. Rather, these strata suggested that unconnected peoples of the past, each with a distinctive flintworking technology, had lived on these various levels at the time they formed." Giddings' two-acre plot yielded thirty artifact-bearing layers that chronicle 12,500 years of human occupation.

Here the story of Kobuk Valley does not end, but begins. Beyond archaeology and sleuthing the past, the present is wondrous as well. Dall sheep dwell in the Baird Mountains. Beaver, muskrat, and otter frequent streams and sloughs and oxbow lakes. You might happen upon a moose, a ptarmigan, or a red fox, or perhaps the more elusive lynx or wolverine. Fred Hirschmann was photographing the sand dunes at midnight when two wolves approached him. "It was one of the most memorable moments I've had in a national park in Alaska," he said, and he has been to them all. Shorebirds arrive from wintering grounds in California, Hawaii, and Central America and lay their eggs on the open tundra. And here, too, are the caribou, the apotheosis of life in the Arctic.

Roughly thirteen major herds of barren-ground caribou live in Alaska, all of them migratory yet none of them entirely predictable. They move between winter feeding grounds and summer calving grounds, flowing over the land like a braided river, following whatever route affords the best snow and wind and insect conditions, moving en masse as though the entire herd were one organism. Some herds number only a few thousand animals, others hundreds of thousands.

Mysteriously, the size of a herd can change significantly over a short period of time. A good example is the Western Arctic Herd which every year migrates through the Kobuk Valley as it has for ages. In the early 1970s, it numbered about 75,000 animals; in the early 1990s, close to 350,000. Nature has a propensity for cycles, especially in the far north, and caribou herds have no doubt cycled for a long time, rising and falling to some rhythm we have yet to understand. Eskimos know about the cycles but they do not ask why. Only the wind knows, they say, and that is enough. The important thing to them is that the herd returns year after year, for they still rely on caribou for meat and clothing, and every fall the Kobuk River is stained with blood as Eskimo fathers, mothers,

Kobuk Valley

Left: *Lenticular clouds create a surreal pattern above the Great Kobuk Sand Dunes. Stretching over twenty-five square miles, this active dune field north of the Arctic Circle has summer temperatures up to one hundred degrees Fahrenheit.* Above: *The wind-sculpted base of a white spruce is exhumed by shifting sands as a clump of grass seeks protection of the stump.*

and children use their skiffs, outboard motors, knives, and rifles to perpetuate what their ancestors have been doing for nearly a thousand generations, perhaps longer. This is subsistence hunting, not sport hunting, and is legal in Kobuk Valley National Park, for hunting is a traditional way of life here. What has changed, and changed significantly, are the hunting methods.

The placid, patient Kobuk averages two or three miles an hour as it flows fifty miles through its namesake valley, westbound toward Kotzebue Sound and the Chukchi Sea. Its tributaries tend to be more swift and rambunctious. One of them, the Salmon River, flowed into national prominence in 1976 with the publication of John McPhee's *Coming Into the Country*. "This was, in all likelihood," penned the writer from New Jersey, "the most isolated wilderness I would ever see."

If only we could all see it, one at a time, treading and paddling with respect so as to leave it pristine for those who follow and for its own sake. What marvelous lessons we would learn. McPhee wrote about Eskimos that "sat around campfires, as we do, telling tales. They repeated the narratives night after night, yet no one ever told someone else's story; a sense of copyright was inherent, and plagiarism was seemingly unknown." And farther along he and his companions "stopped for the night below a bedrock pool, pitching their tents on a sandy bank under woolly mountains whose ridgelines were several thousand feet above the river. The forest now filled in most of the valley floor and went up the slopes maybe three hundred feet. Bear tracks in the sand by the river were eleven inches long, six inches wide." Wilderness indeed.

Four years after McPhee's float trip down the Salmon River, Kobuk Valley National Park was created. One feature he failed to mention, for it lies upstream of the Kobuk's confluence with the Salmon and the route he followed, is perhaps the most unusual feature of all: the Great Kobuk Sand Dunes—twenty-five square miles of concave, U-shaped and crescent-shaped dunes that form the largest active dune field in Arctic North America.

Lying adjacent to the Kobuk River, the dunes rise in places more than one hundred feet, rippled by the wind, blending one into another, mile after mile in a sea of sand. Tem-peratures here can reach one hundred degrees Fahrenheit in the summer and—with windchill—minus one hundred fifty degrees Fahrenheit in the winter. One can only imagine the eloquence McPhee might have mustered upon seeing such a sight, rounding a bend in his kayak and discovering a small Sahara Desert in Northwestern Alaska.

Prevailing easterly winds carried sand out of the Baird and Schwatka mountains, converged with northerly winds, and dropped their cargo, creating the sand dunes we see today. The most impressive crests lie along the western perimeter next to Kavet Creek. *Kavet* is an Eskimo word and means "moving sand." In some places the dunes marched right over spruce trees and killed them, leaving their naked, branchless trunks like tombstones in the sand. Geologists estimate the dunes began forming as early as 150,000 years ago, and, at their peak extent during glacial times, covered a much more extensive part of Northwest Alaska. With wetter conditions today, a good share of the dunes are stabilized and covered by vegetation. Others remain active and plant-free and are a joy to explore barefoot, especially for weary, bootsore travelers.

To foretell the future of the Kobuk Valley is certainly no easier than reconstructing its past. The rivers will flow, the caribou will move, the traditions will endure and with them the tales passed from parents to children to grandchildren. Eskimo hunting and fishing camps will appear and disappear, and schoolchildren from Kotzebue will visit Onion Portage to stand where their ancestors stood and to watch with dark, learning eyes the placid Kobuk River flowing like the ages through a broad valley in arctic Alaska. And if the balance remains, their children will do the same.

Above: *A boreal forest of white spruce and willows lines Kavet Creek as it wanders through Kobuk Valley before joining the Kobuk River.* Right: *Morning mist enshrouds spruce wetlands between Tunutuk and Nakochelik creeks. Across the Baird Mountains to the north, the valley of the Noatak River supports open tundra over all but its lowest reaches.*

■ *Left:* A Siberian aster adds a touch of color to the Little Kobuk Sand Dunes.
■ *Above:* Like an oasis in a desert, willows and cottongrass flourish below a spring whose water source is likely melting ice and snow buried by drifting sands. ■ *Following Pages:* Moose tracks follow the shore of the glassy Kobuk River which flows through the park at a placid two to five miles per hour. Beyond are the Jade Mountains, a southern reach of the Baird Mountains.

■ *Above:* Prevailing winter winds push the Great Kobuk Sand Dunes west-ward against Kavet Creek. Dunes of the Kobuk Valley are relics of drier times in Northwestern Alaska from fourteen thousand to at least twenty-four thousand years ago. Massive continental glaciers spread over much of North America, but strangely left Kobuk Valley ice-free. ■ *Right:* Shifting sands at Hunt River Dunes have buried and reexposed a ghostly forest of white spruce.

Among connoisseurs of the world's great rivers, there is no debate about the importance of such lifelines as the Mississippi, Amazon, Nile, Danube, Volga, or Yangtze. They sustain entire cultures, but pay the price. All but the Amazon have been radically altered and poisoned, and the Amazon's healthy years are numbered. The wilderness they once flowed through is dying, or dead, and the greatness they once symbolized has been redefined to fit human economics and politics. Float down the Noatak River, however, with the clean sky overhead and the open space all around, and you find a greatness nearly eliminated from the face of the earth, for this is Noatak National Preserve, the largest mountain-rimmed wilderness river basin in North America. You may share the view with Native peoples who maintain their traditional ties with the land.

From Mount Igikpak, highest peak in the central Brooks Range, the Noatak flows 450 miles to Kotzebue Sound and Chukchi Sea, into which ten major tributaries and forty named creeks flow. After coursing fifty miles through a mountainous U-shaped valley in Gates of the Arctic National Park, the Noatak runs across a vast, treeless plain and enters a seventy-mile-long section where the contours close around the river in gentle hills and ridges. For six of those miles canyon walls are quite steep, sometimes climbing straight out of the water. Downriver, the Noatak turns south and enters boreal forest, sliding past the village of Noatak, population three hundred, the river basin's only permanent settlement. Eskimos still hunt and fish, but methods have changed. Canoes are replaced by power boats; sled dogs, by snowmobiles.

"Even so, people are part of the tapestry here," says Karen Jettmar, former teacher and park ranger. "I remember paddling around a bend . . . and seeing several people on a nearby hill. I pulled ashore and walked up to them. They were from the village of Noatak and were picking berries. Friendly people. We talked awhile, then everyone went back to picking berries, and I joined them. It was such a quiet, peaceful time, surrounded by beautiful scenery and silence. I felt as if the land itself were speaking, and we were listening."

River of light, river of life: the Noatak flows through wild Alaska. The air is warm one minute, cold the next. Squawls and rainbows appear. A downpour raises the river and floods your camp. Unpack, repack, unpack, repack. Mergansers and scaups flap by. Caribou look up. A spoke of sunlight shines through the clouds and plays on the tundra. Wildflowers nod in the wind, and you curse the cold. When the wind stops, the mosquitoes come out.

In 1885, S. B. McLenegan, a professional engineer and novice canoeist, tried his luck: "No trace of human habitations could be found, and even the hardy waterfowl seemed to have forsaken the region, leaving nothing to remind us of the great and busy world thousands of miles below."

From mid-March 1989 to early January 1990, a young man named Keith Nyitray traveled the complete length of the Brooks Range from Fort McPherson, Canada, west to Kotzebue, Alaska, a distance of sixteen hundred miles. A friend joined him for the first three hundred miles, then dropped out. After that, it was just Nyitray and his dog, Smoke, alone and on foot, traversing the northernmost mountain range in the world. "I wanted to learn more about the land," he said, "to feel more calm inside." He crossed the Continental Divide ten times, fell into rivers twice, suffered frostbite on four fingers, and had ten encounters with bears, including a bluff charge by a sow protecting her young. "The walking man," Natives called him, or "that crazy white guy." Nearing the end of his odyssey, Nyitray was camped along the Noatak River when a wolf came into his camp. "His tail was up, like an alpha male," Nyitray said. "I couldn't believe it." His dog, Smoke, stayed curled next to the campfire as the wolf approached within eight feet and sat down. And there they sat next to the Noatak, man and wolf, staring at each other across the boundaries of fear and misunderstanding. "His eyes glowed green in the fire light," Nyitray said. "It was like looking into eternity."

It takes a great river to flow that far.

Noatak

Left: Upstream from the Kelly River, white spruce silhouetted by sunset are reflected on the mirrored surface of a slough. Above: Upstream from the Noatak, on a gravel bar of the West Cottonwood Creek, rests an ancient piece of bone armour. Federal law prohibits removal of artifacts so important in piecing together the history of human migration to North America.

■ *Left:* The Noatak River drainage receives perhaps twelve to sixteen inches of precipitation a year. Because of permafrost, however, rain and snowmelt cannot soak into the ground and must run off. The river expands over a broad flood plain following heavy rains. ■ *Above:* Almost as quickly as it rises, its subsequent drop reexposes ponds and gravel bars. ■ *Following Pages:* Downstream from Cutler River, the Noatak flows through an open Arctic plain.

■ *Above:* Following instincts as old as the Arctic, a band of caribou swims the Noatak River on their fall migration south. Native people from Noatak Village and Kotzebue come upstream to meet them, taking what they need for winter meat, fat, and clothing. ■ *Right:* Along sheltered river banks of the Noatak and its tributaries, northern red currant thrives. The juicy red berries may be mixed with blueberries and caribou fat to make *aqutuq*—Eskimo ice cream.

S tand on the northwestern coast of Bering Land Bridge National Preserve on the Seward Peninsula and listen to the footfalls of history, for this is a place of beginnings. The first Americans arrived here by crossing a land bridge created when sea level dropped as much as three hundred feet, exposing the floors of the Bering and Chukchi seas, joining Alaska and Siberia.

Where whales migrate today, people migrated ten- to twenty-five thousand years ago at the end of the two million-year-long Pleistocene Epoch. Vast continental glaciers covered most of northern North America and Asia, but not Northwestern Alaska and far eastern Siberia. Land here was ice-free; a refuge, a beginning. Scientists call it Beringia—lands once connected and now separated, still similar in biogeography and human ecology.

With good weather and a good pair of binoculars you can look across the Bering Strait from Lopp Lagoon and see the Diomede Islands and beyond them East Cape, Siberia. Here the sea floor became an open plain, two continents became one. The land bridge opened not once, but several times, each time for thousands of years; nor was it a narrow neck of land, but rather a broad causeway hundreds of miles wide. People probably did not scurry across but moved incrementally, mile by mile, year by year, generation after generation, hunting wildlife and gathering plants as needed. Nor did they travel by land alone, but also by boat, following the southern coasts and arriving as far south as today's Yukon and Kuskokwim river deltas.

Some stayed in Alaska—the Eskimo, Aleut, Athabascan, Tlingit, Haida—while others moved south between icefields and glaciers to colonize the rest of the New World. About ten thousand years ago, the vast glaciers retreated, sea levels climbed, drowning the land bridge, and one continent became two. Add to this, volcanism, an important player in the story of Bering Land Bridge National Preserve, for during a long period of time, the land here erupted with fire. Lava flowed over permafrost and vented as it went, creating geologic features unique to the Arctic. And with each major explosion a veneer of ash settled over the tundra, preserving, as if in a time warp, the vegetation beneath.

"We approached the strait which separates the two great continents of Asia and America," wrote Captain Frederick William Beechey in 1831, "on one of those beautiful still nights . . . when the sky was without a cloud, and when the midnight sun, scarcely his own diameter below the horizon, tinges with a bright hue all the northern circle. Our ship, propelled by an increasing breeze, glided rapidly along a smooth sea, startling from her path flocks of lummes and dovekies, and other aquatic birds, whose flight could, from the stillness of the scene, be traced by the ear to a considerable distance. . . .

"We noticed upon [an island] a considerable village of yourts [skin tents], the largest of any that had as yet been seen. The natives appear to prefer having their dwellings upon the sandy foundation to the main land, probably on account of the latter being swampy, which is the case every where in the vicinity of this inlet and Kotzebue Sound. . . ."

Some things never change. Calm, magical nights still visit this coast. Countless birds swirl over the land and sea, arriving to raise their young in the brief summer. Polar bears patrol the winter sea ice, waiting for seals to surface at breathing holes. More than a dozen species of marine mammals inhabit the rich water, including eight species of whales. And Eskimo hunters and gatherers still live relatively traditional lives despite the pressures of the modern world.

Other things do change. Where the Arctic Circle slices through Bering Land Bridge National Preserve at Cape Espenberg—a southern counterpart to Cape Krusenstern— American archaeologists plot the ground, probe into the past and turn their collars against the wind. In the not-too-distant future, Soviet archaeologists may join them, for a movement is afoot to create an international Beringia park with sister areas in Alaska and Siberia. Once again, then, a bridge will emerge between two continents; this time a bridge of emerging appreciation for our common ancestors and united future.

Bering Land Bridge

Left: *Seward Peninsula evidences much volcanism near Imuruk Lake. Cracks dissect a lava field below Camille Cone. Above: Kamchatka rhododendron blooms on lichen-encrusted lava. It also grows across the Bering Strait on Siberia's Kamchatka Peninsula. Dry land once connected Asia and North America, allowing migration of plants, animals, and humans.*

■ *Left:* The westernmost tip of North America is at Cape Prince of Wales, just west of Bering Land Bridge National Preserve. Big Diomede Island of the Soviet Union is twenty-five miles offshore, while Siberia's mainland is fifty miles across Bering Strait. ■ *Above:* Over flat plains of the Seward Peninsula, Kuzitrin River wends its way toward the Bering Sea. The United States and the Soviet Union are working to create an international park to preserve Beringia.

■ *Above:* On the tundra hills above Serpentine Hot Springs, granite tors display fanciful shapes. The outcrops are eroded remnants of a magma body that cooled and crystallized some seventy million years ago. ■ *Right:* Like apparitions of Stonehenge, the granite towers rise above tiny blossoms of Kamchatka rhododendron. In the valley, approximately 140° water from the hot springs is piped into a covered pool. Visitors may cool it with water from the creek.

From the mouth of the Noatak River, the Alaska coast swings away from mountains toward beaches, lagoons, and hidden human chronology. This is Cape Krusenstern National Monument, the Olduvai Gorge of American Arctic archaeology, where the story of human occupation spreads out horizontally, not vertically, in a remarkable sequence of 114 separate beach ridges, the oldest inland, the youngest near the sea.

Summer throws light across this land, and winter, a cold darkness. From the cape itself, the town of Kotzebue is only forty miles to the southeast. Inupiat Eskimos travel back and forth by boat in summer and snow machine in winter, traversing the ancient hunting, fishing, and whaling grounds of their ancestors. There are no magnificent mountains or splendid waterfalls or emerald forests here, just a low, windswept cape that scythes the Chukchi Sea and points westward toward Siberia.

No doubt the Eskimos had many names for the cape, all of them appropriate, but it was Lieutenant Otto von Kotzebue, sailing for czarist Russia in the early 1800s, who named it Krusenstern in honor of the first Russian admiral to circumnavigate the world. About a century and a half later, in the late 1950s, with the arrival of Professor J. Louis Giddings, the cape's archaeological significance was discovered. Giddings had searched other areas of Northwest Alaska for windows into the past and in 1948 had unearthed a remarkable collection of small chipped flints at Cape Denbigh, south of Krusenstern on Norton Sound, near the village of Shaktoolik. In the years ahead, similar artifacts would be found as far east as Greenland, all belonging to what is today called the Arctic Small Tool tradition of the Denbigh Flint people. It was a beginning, a glimmer. Giddings, hungry for more, found at Cape Krusenstern a window through time more exciting than anything he could have imagined.

For thousands of years storms had pounded the shores here, depositing new gravel beach fronts whenever unusually strong gales washed ashore. As the new beach fronts were created, new generations of people occupied them. Like Sherlock Holmes in a London morgue, Giddings worked his way through the ages, ridge after ridge, unearthing tools, pottery, hearths, artwork, and dwellings. Every major culture was here: the Denbigh Flint people of five thousand years ago, Alaska's first Eskimos; the Choris and Norton people two millenia

later; the Ipiutak Eskimos at the time of Christ; and the travelers of the Western Thule who carried the Eskimo tongue east to Canada and Greenland. But every good story has a twist, and so does this. Mixed among the Krusenstern chronology is evidence of a culture strangely unlike any that came before or after. The evidence suggests they were a whaling people; that perhaps they settled at the cape when whales were abundant and left when the whales left. No one is certain. Giddings called them the "Old Whalers."

Through the years, Cape Krusenstern has changed: some say for the better, some say for the worse. Traditional hunting and gathering survives among local people, such as the Eskimos at Sheshalik at the southern end of the monument. The winter tundra comes alive in summer with flowers and berries and nesting birds. The wolf, wolverine, and red fox make a living here. And Kivalina trout, bearded seal, and beluga whale still feed many a family. But with the opening of the Red Dog Mine to the east, and with the road cut through the monument to access it, modern man has also left a most visible legacy here.

"Often as I walked back across the many ridges at Cape Krusenstern," Professor Giddings wrote in *Ancient Men of the Arctic,* "I speculated about the people who had lived in this particular area. Their summers would have been cold at best, and the winters formidable. Since earliest times they would have occupied themselves mainly with the quest for food, giving attention too, of course, to the essentials of keeping warm: adequate shelter and clothing. . . . And from all of the people who lived on these beach ridges, sharing similar problems and hardships, there emerged through the centuries the Eskimo of today: a careful, watchful, fun-filled individual—crafty, brave and enduring."

Left: Cloud niagaras from the Chukchi Sea flow over Ingitkalik Mountain and billow off Krusenstern Lagoon. Above: Flora Green uses her ulu to clean dried strips of oogruk, or bearded seal. Bountiful Cape Krusenstern provides oogruk, beluga whale, arctic char, whitefish, seal oil, and many other foods consumed during the long months of winter.

■ *Left:* Limestone outcrops on the west slope of Ingitkalik Mountain above Krusenstern Lagoon. A thin strip of land toward the horizon separates the lagoon from the open waters of the Chukchi Sea. Nearby, some 114 former beach ridges contain an unparalleled chronology of human use over many thousands of years. ■ *Above:* Farther north, the shore of Kotlik Lagoon creates stark patterns. Snowdrifts in the lee of the bluffs may linger through summer.

■ *Above:* Dale Ahnangnatoguk and Gary Kanchell sit below a sled stored on a spit of land running between Tukrok River and Cape Krusenstern. Above the boys are strips of beluga whale muktuk awaiting boiling. ■ *Right:* A solitary blossom of villous cinquefoil appears in a bed of rock jasmine on tundra adjacent to the Chukchi Sea and Kiligmak Inlet. Late June through mid-July marks the peak of summer bloom at Cape Krusenstern National Monument.

■ *Left:* A glaucous gull feather rests on the Arctic Ocean beach near the mouth of Agagrak Creek. Unlike ocean beaches in temperate climes, shores of the Arctic Ocean remain largely unpolluted by plastic wastes. ■ *Above:* The midnight sun skirts the horizon beyond the mouth of Agagrak Creek. Although there is an illusion of vast wilderness beyond, hidden by the bluff and just three miles away is a huge shipping port for lead and zinc ore from Red Dog Mine.

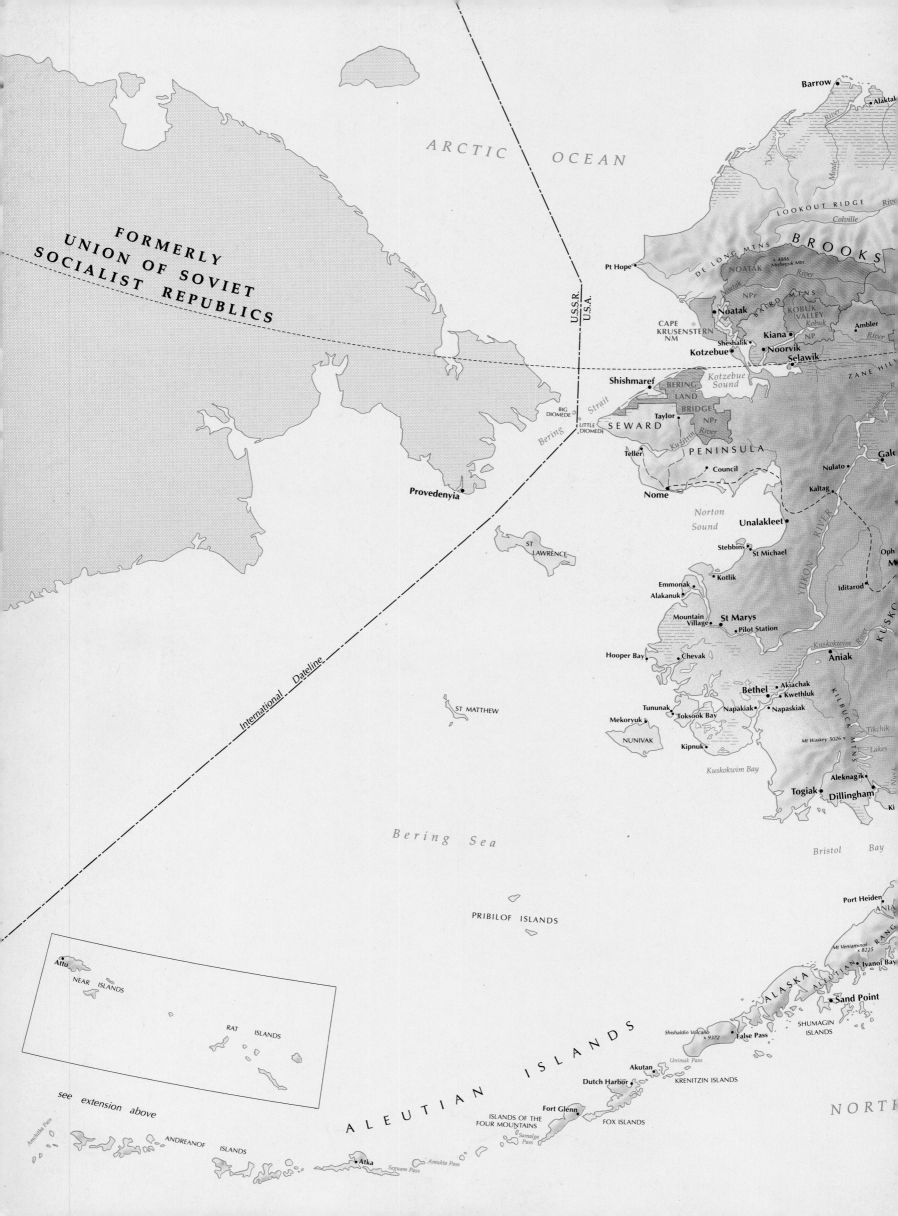

ARCTIC OCEAN

FORMERLY
UNION OF SOVIET
SOCIALIST REPUBLICS

U.S.S.R.
U.S.A.

Barrow
Alaktak

LOOKOUT RIDGE
Colville
River

BROOKS

DE LONG MTNS
NOATAK
x 4886 Misheguk Mtn
BAIRD MTNS

Pt Hope

Noatak
Kobuk
KOBUK
VALLEY
NP
Ambler

CAPE
KRUSENSTERN
NM
Kiana
Sheshalik
Noorvik
Kotzebue
Selawik

ZANE HILV

Shishmaref
Kotzebue
Sound

Bering
Strait
BERING
LAND
BRIDGE
NPr

BIG
DIOMEDE
Taylor
Kuzitrin River

LITTLE
DIOMEDE
SEWARD

Teller
PENINSULA
Gale

Council
Nulato

Provedenyia
Nome
Kaltag

Norton
Sound
Unalakleet

Stebbins
St Michael
YUKON RIVER
Oph
M

ST
LAWRENCE
Kotlik
Iditarod

Emmonak
Alakanuk

Mountain
Village
St Marys
Pilot Station

Hooper Bay
Chevak
Kuskokwim River
KUSKO

Aniak

Bethel
Akiachak
Kwethluk

ST MATTHEW
Tununak
Napakiak
Napaskiak
KILBUCK MTNS
Tikchik

Mekoryuk
Toksook Bay
Lakes

Kipnuk
Mt Waskey 5026 x

NUNIVAK

Kuskokwim Bay
Aleknagik

Togiak
Dillingham
Ki

Bering Sea

Bristol Bay

International Dateline

PRIBILOF ISLANDS

Port Heiden
ANI
RANG

Mt Veniaminof
x 8225
Ivanof Bay

Attu
NEAR ISLANDS

ALASKA
ALEUTIAN RANGE
Sand Point

RAT ISLANDS
SHUMAGIN
ISLANDS

Shishaldin Volcano
x 9372
False Pass

ALEUTIAN ISLANDS
NORTH

see extension above
Akutan
Unimak Pass
KRENITZIN ISLANDS

Dutch Harbor

Amchitka Pass
ANDREANOF
ISLANDS
Fort Glenn
ISLANDS OF THE
FOUR MOUNTAINS
Samalga
Pass
FOX ISLANDS

Atka
Seguam Pass
Amukta Pass

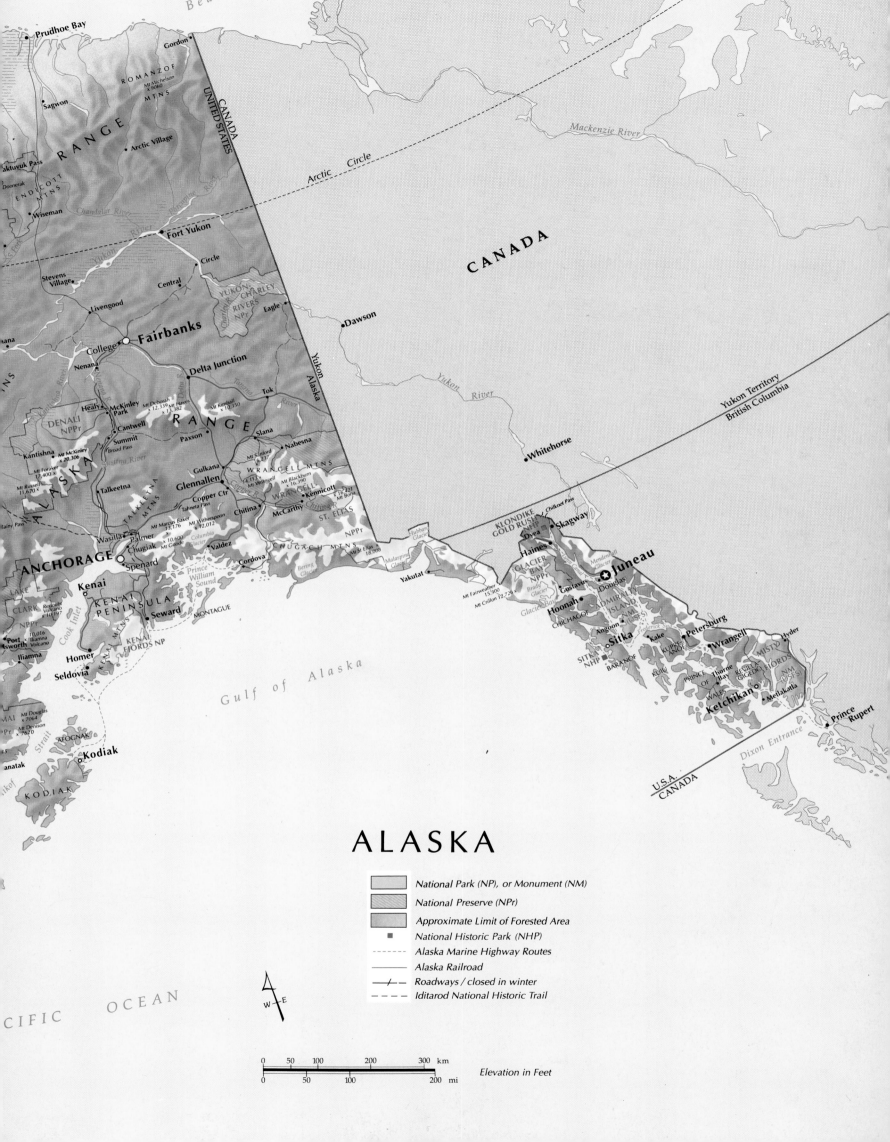

ALASKA

National Park (NP), or Monument (NM)

National Preserve (NPr)

Approximate Limit of Forested Area

National Historic Park (NHP)

Alaska Marine Highway Routes

Alaska Railroad

Roadways / closed in winter

Iditarod National Historic Trail

Elevation in Feet

| 0 | 50 | 100 | 200 | 300 km |
| 0 | 50 | 100 | 200 mi | |

Beaufort Sea

Prudhoe Bay
Gordon
Sagwon
ROMANZOF
MT'S
Mt Michelson
x 9060
R A N G E
Arctic Village
aktuvuk Pass
Doonerak
ENDICOTT
MTNS
Wiseman
CANADA
UNITED STATES

Mackenzie River

CANADA

Arctic Circle

Chandalar River
Stevens Village
Fort Yukon
Circle
Central
YUKON- CHARLEY
RIVERS NPr
Eagle
Livengood
Fairbanks
College
Nenana
Dawson
Delta Junction
Tok
Healy
McKinley Park
Mt Deborah x 12,339
Mt Hayes x 13,182
Mt Kimball x 10,750
DENALI NPPr
Cantwell
Summit
Broad Pass
Paxson
Slana
Nabesna
Mt Sanford x 16,237
WRANGELL MTNS
Kantishna
Mt McKinley x 20,306
Mt Foraker x 17,400
Gulkana
Mt Wrangell 14,163
Mt Blackburn x 16,390
Whitehorse
Yukon River
Alaska
Yukon River
Mt Russell 11,670 x
Talkeetna
Glennallen
Copper Ctr
Kennicott
Mt Bona 16,421
WRANGELL
ST. ELIAS
Chitina
McCarthy
Mt Marcus Baker 13,176
Mt Witherspoon x 12,012
Wasilla
Palmer
Chugiak
Mt Gerdine
Spenard
Columbia Glacier
Valdez
NPPr
CHUGACH MTNS
Cordova
Hubbard Glacier
Bering Glacier
Malaspina Glacier
Yakutat
Mt St Elias 18,008

ANCHORAGE
Kenai
KENAI PENINSULA
Seward
Prince William Sound
MONTAGUE
LAKE CLARK NPPr
Redoubt Volcano 10,016
Iliamna Volcano 10,016
Port worth
Iliamna
Homer
Seldovia
KENAI FJORDS NP
KENAI MTNS

Gulf of Alaska

Mt Fairweather 15,300
Mt Crillon 12,728 x
KLONDIKE GOLD RUSH
Dyea
Skagway
Haines
GLACIER BAY NPPr
Mendenhall Glacier
Juneau
Douglas
Gustavus
Hoonah
CHICHAGOF
ADMIRALTY ISLAND NM
Angoon
Sitka
SITKA NHP
BARANOF
Kake
Petersburg
ANGF
KUPR
KUIU
PRINCE OF Thorne Bay
WALES
Wrangell
Hyder
REVILLA GIGEDO
MISTY FJORDS NM
USFS
Ketchikan
Metlakatla
Prince Rupert
Dixon Entrance
U.S.A. CANADA

Yukon Territory
British Columbia

MT
Mt Douglas x 7064
Pr
Mt Denison x 7620
AFOGNAK
Kodiak
KODIAK
Shelikof Strait
anatak

PACIFIC OCEAN

N
W E

Acknowledgements

High above Thorofare Pass in Denali National
Park, a green auroral curtain graces the northeastern sky. Although threats from a burgeoning
population loom beyond the horizon, we still
celebrate what has been preserved in Alaska's
magnificent national parks! Our heartfelt thanks
go to the following Alaskans who assisted
in our celebration, the creation of this book:

Ken Adkisson • Allen and Mary Ahnangnatoguk
Dale Ahnangnatoguk • Glen and Patty Alsworth
Gary Archer • Mike Archer
Marcia Arnold • Lee Anne Ayres
Ray Bane • Reneé Beymer
Cheryl Bloethe • Paul Brewster
Larry and Karla Bright • William E. Brown
Will Cameron • Gary Candelaria
Stan Carrick • Anne Castellina
Don Chase • Glenn Clark
Bruce Dale • Laurie DeWispelaere
Deanna Dulen • Carolyn Elder
Alan Eliason • Jim Eshenower
Boyd Evison • Peter Fitzmaurice
Bernd and Pat Gaedeke • Jeff Gnass
Amos and Flora Green • Andy Greenblatt
Karen Gustin •Jay Hammond
Jim Hannah • Jeff and Karen Hansen
Rich Harris • Roger Harritt
Melanie Heacox • Andy Hutchinson
Kent Jackson • Bob Jacobsen
Karen Jettmar • Gary Kanchel
Earl Kingik • Dan Klaes
Penny and Dennis Knuckles • Chuck Lennox
Rosalie McCreary • Janis Meldrum
Dave Mills • Ken Mitchell
David Nemeth • Keith Nyitray
Jim Okonek • Sally Orot
Bruce Paige • Sonny Petersen
Dale Pihlman • Dick Proenneke
John Quinley • Bud Rice
Krisanne Rice • Bill Roberts
Kate Roney-Faulkner • Richard Sage
Mike and Barbara Shallcross • Roger Siglin
Kim Speckman • Richard Steele
George Stroud • Matthew Sturm
Ernie Suazo • Ronald W. Sutton
Rebecca Talbot • Lowell Thomas, Jr.
Hollis Twitchell • Steve Ulvi
Larry and Gail Van Slyke • Jonathan Waterman